ART EDUCATION: SENIOR HIGH SCHOOL

Art Education
Senior High School

Written by a Task Force of specialists in senior high school art education.
Task Force Chairman: Angela G. Paterakis

The National Art Education Association
1916 Association Drive
Reston, Virginia 22091

10 • 1M • 884

ISBN 0–937652–04–0

TASK FORCE CHAIRMAN:
Angela G. Paterakis
Chairman
Division of Art Education
The School of the Art Institute of Chicago
Chicago, Illinois

MEMBERS OF THE TASK FORCE
Roy E. Abrahamson
Professor-in-Charge of Art Education
    Graduate Studies
School of Art
Southern Illinois University
Carbondale, Illinois

John Almquist
Chairman
Department of Art
North Shore Country Day School
Winnetka, Illinois

Carmen Armstrong
Assistant Professor of Art Education
Northern Illinois University
DeKalb, Illinois

Sharon Bocklage
Aesthetic Education Program
CEMREL, Inc.
St. Ann, Missouri

Wesley Buchwald
Art Consultant
Chicago Public Schools
Chicago, Illinois

Suzanne Cohan
Supervisor of Art
Office of the Superintendent of
    Public Instruction
State of Illinois
Springfield, Illinois

Beverly Jeanne Davis
Managing Editor
National Art Education Association
Washington, D.C.

Kenneth Englund
Illinois Arts Council
Chicago, Illinois

Ruth Esserman
Chairman
Department of Fine Arts
Highland Park High School
Highland Park, Illinois

Truman Fox
Art Department
Lyons Township High School
La Grange, Illinois

Jeannette Gaumond
Art Department
Lyons Township High School
La Grange, Illinois

Royce Lewis
Chairman
Department of Art
Evanston Township High School
Evanston, Illinois

Hazel Loew
Niles East High School
Skokie, Illinois

Nadine J. Meyers
Aesthetic Education Program
CEMREL, Inc.
St. Ann, Missouri

Jean Mary Morman
Associate Professor of Art
Loyola University
Chicago, Illinois

Hector Munoz
Art Teacher
Lyons Township High School
La Grange, Illinois

Lou Ann Musinski
Art Department
Oak Park-River Forest High School
Oak Park, Illinois

Helen Patton
Consultant in Art, K-12
Racine Unified Schools
Racine, Wisconsin

Arthur Pelz
Chairman, Dept. of Art
Oak Park-River Forest High School
Oak Park, Illinois

Helen Ratzer
Museum Education
Museum of Contemporary Art
Chicago, Illinois

Don Seiden
Associate Professor of Art and
    Art Education
Department of Teacher Education
The School of the Art Institute of
    Chicago
Chicago, Illinois

Jerry L. Truesdell
Art Teacher
Greeley West High School
Greeley, Colorado

Sue Warren
Art Teacher
Oak Park-River Forest High School
Oak Park, Illinois

Ephraim Weinberg
Chairman
Department of Teacher Education
The School of the Art Institute of
    Chicago
Chicago, Illinois

Byron Young
OE Fellow
U.S. Office of Education
Washington, D.C.

Contents

Chapter I   **INTRODUCTION**   1

Art and the Individual, the Culture, and the Community   3

The Outcomes of the Senior High School Art Program   6

Chapter II   **ART IN SENIOR HIGH SCHOOL EDUCATION**   9

Historical Survey and Emerging Trends   11

Some Strategies for the Teaching of Art   19
    The Student-Centered Approach   21
    Interdisciplinary Studies   24
    Art Approached Behaviorally   31
    Art Approached as Perception   35
    Art Approached Experientially   38
    The Artist as Model   42
    Art History in the High School Art Program   44

Chapter III   **ART IN THE SCHOOL AND THE COMMUNITY**   51

Art in the Secondary School   53
    Who Teaches Art?   54
    Time, Space, and Numbers in the Senior High School
        Art Program   61
    Change in Art Education   65
    Who Pays for Art Education?   69

Art in the Community   75
    The Artist as a Resource   76

The Art Museum   81
The Art Mobile Experience   86
The School-without-Walls   88
The School Within the School   90
Art Education in Small Communities   95
Careers in Art   98

Chapter I
INTRODUCTION

Art and the Individual, the Culture, and the Community

The growing national concern for the quality of life and the obligation which confronts educational systems make it imperative that art play a more dominant role in the education of the student. The National Art Education Association is dedicated to the goal of a quality art program for all students at every level of instruction. The requirements for quality art education at each level vary to some extent, but there are commonalities of purpose for the teaching of art which can be directed to every student.

> *Art in the school is both a body of knowledge and a series of activities which the teacher organizes to provide experiences related to specific goals. The sequence and depth of these experiences are determined by the nature of the art discipline, the objectives desired, and by the interests, abilities, and needs of children at different levels of growth.*[1]

The broad parameters for the rationale of the teaching of art are based on the relationship between art and the individual, art and the community, and art and the culture. Each of these categories provides the basis for determining the goals of a quality art program at given levels of instruction.

> *Art and the Individual:*
> *Both when he produces works of art and when he contemplates them, man uses the arts to help him understand himself and the world around him. One of the traditional and unique functions of the arts has been to emphasize individual interpretation and expression.*[2]

Our society has put so much emphasis upon technological development that the individual and his uniqueness have been minimized in the process. Individual identity, self-esteem, and self-accomplishment are imperative if our society is to grow and flourish.

A primary aim of art education for the senior high school student should be to help him to be able to participate in and enjoy aesthetic experiences, in the natural world, in works of art, and in the creation of his own art expressions. The ability to become personally and directly involved in such experiences provides personal growth and sensitivity which can enrich and deepen his everyday life.

Art education should contribute toward the development of an individual who is aesthetically responsible in the decisions he makes concerning the community and should contribute to its improvement.

Acceptance of this responsibility is particularly important during periods of rapid technological development and social change.[3]

Art and the Culture:
The visual arts contain a record of the achievement of mankind, since the values and beliefs of a people are uniquely manifested in the art forms they produce. A critical examination of these forms can lead to a better understanding of both past and present cultures,[4]

and serve to maintain and extend the existing culture. Ours is a young nation which, in the last century, has initiated an art tradition which is uniquely American and is not merely an extension of another tradition. The student, if he is to identify with our nation's needs and possibilities, must become aware and informed of our cultural heritage and its contemporary manifestations.

The high school art program should help him personally experience as well as understand art expressions of other cultures as well as his own, thus contributing to his appreciation of his cultural heritage and the meaning it can have in his own personal life, and broadening his realm of aesthetic experience.

The visual arts today continue to be a means whereby man attempts to give form to his ideas and feelings and to gain personal satisfaction through individual accomplishment.[5]

Art education in the schools provides one vehicle by which these opportunities are systematically introduced and reinforced over a period of years.

The growing complexity of our contemporary culture, including its visual aspects, also requires of every individual a capacity for visual discrimination and judgment which the art program provides.[6]

From direct involvement in the visual and sensuous qualities of works of art, and from deepening aesthetic experiences, the high school student should develop both discriminating judgment and a greater capacity for the enjoyment of art objects as well as of the natural and man-made environment.

Art and the Community:
Through the ages man has used the arts to build and enrich his environment. Art experiences should help him understand the visual

4

qualities of these environments and lead to the desire and the ability to improve them.

An art education program which consistently emphasizes the ability to make qualitative visual judgments can help each student to assume his share of responsibility for the improvement of the aesthetic dimension of personal and community living.[7]

The high school art program should contribute to the student's awareness of and responsibility for his personal and community environment and its aesthetic qualities.

It should lead to his more aware and discriminating judgment as a consumer, to his ability to personally relate to works of arts which comprise his cultural heritage, and to his capacity to communicate with the world through aesthetic experience.

REFERENCES

1 *The Essentials of a Quality School Art Program: A Position Statement by the National Art Education Association,* Washington, D.C.
2 *Ibid.*
3 *Ibid.*
4 *Ibid.*
5 *Ibid.*
6 *Ibid.*
7 *Ibid.*

Outcomes of the Senior High School Art Program

A quality art program should result in an increase in the student's capacity to:

1. Have intense involvement in and response to personal visual experiences.[1] *The art experience provides the activities which are valued by the individual intrinsically. Both the production of an art object and the ability to view a work of art with insight are means of achieving intense personal involvement.*

In secondary education, creating and producing an art object develops sharper visual acuity and further intensifies personal visual experiences. Being able to experience more deeply leads to a greater comprehension of the visual and sensuous qualities of an object.

2. Perceive and understand visual relationships in the environment.[2] *The development of a visually literate student who can make informed visual judgments about man-made objects or natural phenomena becomes an important outcome for every art program.*

Through continued studies of existing things in the environment and their relationship to need and function, the high school student can develop an intense understanding. Informed visual judgments through constant observations set the pattern for the student as a future consumer and can guide him into achieving a desirable quality of life.

3. Think, feel, and act creatively with visual art materials.[3] *The process of transforming the materials of the artist into a whole work of art is an integral part of every art program. The creative process, the manner in which an artist produces a work of art, engages the student at every level. The variations of approach applied to this process and the materials and media used to implement it provide many ways for the student to express himself.*

At the secondary level, art processes are continually explored with new dimensions and insights contributed by the student and the teacher. New media can become a constant challenge to the variety of forms created. Along with the making of the work of art, the processes of selecting and experimenting are heightened.

4. Increase manipulative and organizational skills in art performance appropriate to his abilities.[4] The development of skills is an important outcome for every student. Certain processes and techniques are unique to the visual arts and provide content for instruction. The method by which one constructs a pot in clay, or the process by which a design can be replicated by the use of silk screen, are skills which may be developed as part of instruction in art.

Refinement of techniques and greater control of the visual art processes are essential at the secondary level. The ability to create a work of art requires the knowledge of "how" and "what." Technical skills and knowledge coupled with principles and elements of design (organization) are needed for the student to achieve a fully realized art form.

5. Acquire a knowledge of man's visual art heritage.[5] The records of man's accomplishments through the ages lives because of the arts! This foundation of ideas can be introduced at all levels via films, slides, works of art in school or by visiting museums and artists, etc. Youngsters can begin to see connections between what has happened in the arts, ways in which different people have lived, and what they are trying to make and do in their own lives.

At the secondary level, emphasis on the study of differences that exist in man's art heritage—relationships between man and his own cultural influences, and the forces of ethnic distinctions add to a broader understanding of man to man and man to his world.

6. Use art knowledge and skills in his personal and community life.[6] As students grow, they must begin to assume responsibility for their own actions, personally and publicly. This will manifest itself in a heightened sensitivity to, and ability to function in, their physical and psychological environment.

At the secondary level, career opportunities in art should be considered as part of the art offerings. The student who is interested in art should realize the uniqueness of art in contrast to other disciplines.

7. Understanding the nature of art and the creative process.[7] Through art, students are involved with creative visual expression. The creative process promotes acts of originality, fluency, and flexibility. A body of knowledge exists in art in an historical and philosophical context which becomes the basis for sounding or investigating the nature of art and the creative process.

The high school student needs to understand the unique nature of art as a creative process in contrast to other aspects of the school course offerings. He should come to realize the values of art in the development of personal awareness and responsiveness, the ability to form and execute one's own ideas and feelings, and the fostering of good judgment and critical observation.

REFERENCES
1 *The Essentials of a Quality School Art Program: A Position Statement by the National Art Education Association,* Washington, D.C.
2 *Ibid.*
3 *Ibid.*
4 *Ibid.*
5 *Ibid.*
6 *Ibid.*
7 *Ibid.*

Chapter II
ART IN SENIOR HIGH SCHOOL EDUCATION

Historical Survey and Emerging Trends

Where are we? Where are we going? Where have we been? It is not at all surprising that art educators of the early 70's should feel compelled to take stock of the directions in which the field is moving. In an ever changing discipline, recent years have seen a spectacular number of new programs, varying emphases, physical rearrangements, and innovations in the teaching of art in the public schools.

The changes sometimes reflect changes in the total educational system and in our technological society. In a way, education has been everyman's heyday. The continuum of those who express ideas about education extends from the vocal but non-involved critic to the blindly involved educator doing his thing at the grass roots level. Educators have reflectively, and at times impulsively, responded to the expressions of critics; and a great variety of approaches is the result. The art field is no exception.

The person who steps out of his busy involvement for a moment to take a look at the past, present and future of art education might well respond "Hold on!" Perhaps that is what those who allocate funds for us to "do our thing" with their children in schools are thinking as they hear an enthusiastic, though somewhat contradictory, chorus of acclamations. What do they hear? What do they conclude? It behooves us to listen to what we have said and are saying.

In surveying the current situation in secondary art education, one can start with the first examples of "art education" in formal education, and proceed toward present day practices, dismissing the past on the basis that replacement of one emphasis constitutes an improvement on, and rejection of, the former. Acceptance of this avenue of thinking can clear the way for anyone who steps to the soap box to declare a new "saving" approach. Encouragement to innovate only adds fuel to such fires. In a society geared to planned obsolescence, to admit accepting parts of old approaches as valid is to flirt with scorn. But *must* the validity of new goals be accompanied by what Michael Day recently phrased as the "graceful demise of earlier rationales"?[1]

Certainly we see vestiges of numerous past rationales in art education today—some which we tolerate, some which we support, and some which we reject. How many practices do we accept which seem compatible with current needs and at the same time contain disguised remnants of old positions merely stripped of their original *raison d'être*? Are there some basic principles on which earlier rationales for art education were built which are broad enough to support adaptions to "today"? Is this a time to continue shattering our front by new or personal terminology, or to sort, organize, and take account of our superfluous verbiage?

The task of taking a comprehensive view of past trends and prevailing emphases in secondary level art education is complicated.

ART FOR THE ELITE

In the United States prior to a public school commitment to art for the adolescent, art education did exist for young men and women. The rationale for art training for cultured young ladies was that this added, genteel accomplishment would provide a girl with the ability to make drawings suitable to bring pleasure to friends as gifts (Edgeworth). It was not intended that the young ladies should develop competencies comparable to serious artists-in-training.

Likewise, the non-art purpose of spare-time drawing instruction for young gentlemen, was to be able to more quickly and specifically describe objects about which they may be communicating—part of a proper education (Locke). William Morris Hunt was one of the first to conceive of art as a part of education in a more inclusive way. His interpretation of "art for the public" was art discussion as part of the enhanced background of the upper class leading to their ability to appreciate art, and he did welcome those with non-vocational interests.

Today, with public education available to all, and art officially included in the curriculum, it would seem that this idea of art for the elite has been replaced. However, though officially denounced, there are numerous situations where art for the elite or for "refinement" exists in some form. It is not uncommon for the college-bound high school student to get the required "solid subjects" taken care of first and then take art if time remains—much the same kind of value system dictating priorities as that expressed in the 1690's by John Locke.[2]

> *I do not mean that I would have your Son a* perfect Painter . . . *will require more time than a young Gentleman can spare from his other Improvements of greater Moment.*

It is still too common for comfort to hear of art as one of the frills.

We may not be able to avoid what seems to be another vestige of the art for the elite trend. The clustering of people of similar economic status forms school districts which value and can afford to support to varying degrees, the expensive "frills." According to Coleman, recent studies support the conclusions of his famous 1966 report; and the family status and value system of the peer group influenced by the community are important in what students achieve. He writes:[3]

> *All factors considered, the most important variable–in or out of school–in a child's performance remains his family's educational background. The second most important factor is the educational background, the social-class background, of the families of the children in the school.*

The cycle of values, experience, and support for those things appreciated leads to inequalities of opportunities across communities in art education.

Art can still exist in our schools as a cultural nicety—the Sunday Supplement for some who do not ascribe to education solely as preparation for "work," but who do not recognize the conceptual nature of art learning. In other instances, money allocated to school trips to studios or museums is among those fringe areas which are funded or not as the budget fluctuates. Even when trips are feasible and supported, however, we take "now" oriented high school students to museums which by the very nature of physical arrangements, restrictions, and mode of presentation, have an aura of democratically allowing exposure to "class" art. To deny this is to deny reality, but to condone it is to contradict what most recent art educators promote, i.e., equal opportunity in art for all.

APPRECIATION OF "BEAUTY"

To some, the words "art" and "beauty" are synonymous . . . and neither can really be defined. A look at what people have been educated to call "beauty" explains the confusion. In 1870 William Cullen Bryant believed that art should be taught for appreciation of beauty, with art being defined as a moral and social teacher. The picture study of that time was intended to refine taste, develop appreciation, and uplift the spirit. Earlier historical paintings and educational and moral paintings were the "correct" mode of Benjamin West's Academy. Beauty took on other definitions as the influence of Clive Bell, Arthur Dow, and William Morris spread. Stylized plant motifs were carefully copied and arranged in school art classes. The first decade or two of the 20th century saw a philosophical conflict over beauty between Hegel, and Dewey, who saw beauty in reality. The Bauhaus introduced a new kind of beauty in the honest use of materials contributing an aesthetic quality to the immediate environment. Unfortunately, when these ideas reached the level of application in the school, a lack of recognition of purpose for art as a required course in high schools led to consumer arts courses in the 1930's which amounted to acquiring a "polite accomplishment" again.

No longer do we copy proper shapes—the plant motifs, derived from geometric shapes; but many art teachers operate as Bell advocated, sharpening sensitivity to elements of design and composition, in introductory courses especially, and take the approach as much for granted as did those who promoted exercises in copying beautiful forms and designing borders.

We continue to attempt to facilitate the students' process of forming aesthetic judgments mainly through discussion. The means may vary from the cognitive emphasis of art history and art appreciation courses to the affective emphasis of being daily exposed to the life style and work of an artist-in-residence.

Social comment is common in the art work to which secondary level students are exposed. While art teachers may avoid making moral judgments about the art they present, students confronted with an enlarged spectrum of situations in art forms do make such judgments along with the artistic qualitative analysis.

ART FOR COMMUNICATION

Benjamin Franklin in 1770, extolled the usefulness of art training as being valuable for communicating. Locke, influenced by Franklin, advocated drawing as time permitted, for essentially the same reasons. Francis Parker in 1874 referred to art as being one mode of expression, and Horace Mann felt that communication could be improved by developing the ability to draw in addition to writing.

The emphasis of the child study movement of the late 19th century—the child's self-expression—recurred in Lowenfeld's and other child-centered educators' writings.

"Self-expression" is a term which we tend to use with little critical examination. Does it mean mere communication—a child's statements of interests, attitudes, ideas, and feelings? Is it release? Is exposure of a subliminal "self" implied? Is it meant that a child introspects and projects this mature awareness? Art educators today find their own definitions of "self-expression" somewhere along a continuum with these as a result of the influence of Freudian psychology on art and Viktor Lowenfeld's interest in personality growth and self-adjustment through art. The related one-time emphasis on emotional release led to some assumptions that art works of children could contribute to the teacher's insight into the child's inner world. Inherent problems of misinterpretation and gross ignoring of other possibly influential variables has subjected this position to criticism. Yet, it seems to have caught on in people's minds enough that one can still hear "emotional release," "self-awareness," or opportunity for teacher's "insight" into pupil behavior as purposes for art education.

Collingwood, the English philosopher, has provided for some art teachers a palatable position. He accepts the idea that art is communication by the artist to his elite, or special audience, which can share his personal view of reality. Therefore the artist's emphasis of that aspect of reality to which he personally responds, becomes his individual expression, which also is assumed to communicate; with this interpretation, there is room in art education for both the viewpoints of individual interpretations of the self, of concerns, of society, and of compositions of any sort, and the purpose of art as communication. In addition, the figural content of art offers an alternate mode of expression to the written or spoken word, to numerical symbols, or to gestures and movement.

VISUAL PERCEPTUAL DEVELOPMENT

Visual awareness is a primary movement to encourage a student to acquire visual information without which a significant visual synthesis—an individual's statement—cannot emerge. Most present statements of purpose at the secondary art level for both the general education art courses and specific studio courses include some recognition of this purpose. Emphasis upon dealing with specific visual information in various ways is aimed to develop the ability to selectively incorporate those qualities which contribute to the specificity of the total statement.

Probably most evidence of visual perceptual development is requested in the form of drawings—directly, and as recalled from nature. Kimon Nicholaides inspired approaches that are commonly used to demonstrate visual understanding of form. One associates the name of Rudolf Arnheim with visual perceptual development. Certainly his extensive study has been most influential recently, but others before him also attended to the benefits of developing visual literacy to some degree.

As part of the greater sensory awareness movement, one recalls emphases upon seeing type forms in nature, and the manipulation of concrete forms in Froebel's Kindergarten. In the early 1800's, Alcott valued drawing from nature for its contribution to the imagination. Later, emphasis was placed upon recognition of particular forms in one's real environment. Horace Mann felt that observation led to awareness and to the ability to communicate. Diverging further from the practical, Dewey maintained that awareness of unique aspects of experience was basic to the aesthetic response.

The simple practice of drawing from observation for developing eye-hand coordination has been dropped from most current statements of rationale. However, interest in the psychomotor domain of human behavior would suggest general recognition of this area. This approach may yet be involved in some way in art education's formal emphases. It is a reality in practice, but at a more sophisticated level than when the "eye-hand coordination" phrase was coined.

CREATIVE DEVELOPMENT

Creativity has so long been associated with art—and for so many varying purposes—that many avoid reference to it, at least by that name. Arthur Dow even referred to creative power as a divine gift, and today "artistic talent" is still used to describe something some people have that others do not. Cizek believed that creativity existed in *every* child. "Creative" has also been equated to art appreciation—a practice supposedly developed by the early academic drawing exercises.

Teaching methodology of the child-centered groups was to produce the creative child. Shaeffer-Simmern relied on memory and repetition of tasks to let

15

creativity unfold and to bring forth changes in his subject's visual configurations. Others advocate a breadth of experiences as a basis for creative production.

Confusion about creativity called for redefinition. J. P. Guilford gave clarity to the concept of creativity by identifying the levels of intellectual operations, convergent and divergent production, associated with creativity. Tests for the various components of the structure of the intellect model gave validity to the theoretical position. Guilford's statement that creativity could most likely be encouraged in the arts in schools gave impetus to a fresh emphasis.

Lowenfeld also saw art as being instrumental to the creative process. Belief in the unique creative potential of the individual was the pivotal element in creative problem solving at the Bauhaus. Dewey, identifying the inquiry stages in the creative problem solving process, contributed to the creativity emphasis in secondary art education geared to individualization.

Some reference to creativity remains in most statements of purpose. More emphasis on recognition of the creative inquiry process is emerging as teachers seek alternatives to teacher-oriented goals.

PRE-PROFESSIONAL TRAINING

The degree of specialization available within the area of art suggests some commitment on the part of some schools to the preparation of artists. If financial resources permit, in depth experience is frequently available in whatever studio expertise is represented on the faculty.

Walter Smith saw the high school level as the culmination of his progressive developmental stages where preprofessional training was appropriate. The 1920's saw in high school art a watered-down art school emphasis on drawing and painting. Drawing from casts may be replaced by drawing guitars in our awakened sensitivity to student interests, but the ends may differ little.

Following the model of the Bauhaus, in districts able to afford the luxury, one can find materials and equipment which encourage a student to specialize. Some college studio instructors seem to want incoming students to have such focus and experience. Others question it as being narrowing to the student. Vincent Lanier maintains that training the artist is a "minimal portion of the obligation of those who teach art in the schools."[4]

Bruner would support examining the behavioral structure of the creative artist and encouraging the behavior characteristics of his inquiry process. Perhaps this use of the artist-in-residence, as now has gained impetus, would be valid.

Work-study programs, high school commercial art courses, and apprenticeships also exist and may increase if more states legislate their concern that high school students graduate with some saleable skill.

CRAFT

Like the word "creativity," "craft" is subject to various interpretations, and therefore communicating becomes difficult without definition. Art history texts may treat painting, sculpture, and architecture separately, and lump other arts into a "minor arts" section. Sculpture studios sometimes are categorized as belonging within a crafts domain with courses in weaving, jewelry, and ceramics.

The variation in interpretation comes from the past emphases on physical control and the theoretical separation of fine and functional products. Muscular control and skill development were emphasized by Walter Smith, penmanship by Horace Mann, and accurate drawing through eye-hand coordination by Peter Schmidt, before the mid-1800's.

But Emerson in his 1841 essays asked that the distinction between fine and useful arts be forgotten. In the Bauhaus and public school art influenced by this school, the union of arts and crafts became a reality. Commercial interests have capitalized on the openness of the art product concepts and offer a dazzling variety of materials, media, and processes for the high school art student.

MATERIALS EXPLORATION

New directions may lead to unpredicted avenues and difficulty in remaining unconfused about purpose. The thrill of discovering the possibilities of materials has in some high school teaching clouded the role of media as means to more defensible ends.

The novelty of unconventional materials was used as a "come-on" in required art classes of the 1930's. However, the exploration advocated by D'Amico was tempered by the aim of creative achievement using the teacher as a materials and technical guidance resource. Aims such as experience with materials to ascertain essential qualities to classify by forms and to discover truth through application and manipulation sound similar to those of experientialists today.

CONCEPTUAL APPROACH

Much of art education today apparently is a composite of art educators' thinking about past directions in relation to today's needs. Concepts about art are examined, and advocates of the conceptual approach would divorce themselves from a base of materials, or elements-of-art, and proceed from a concepts-about-art approach. This in itself is not entirely new, either, as Horace Mann saw art as contributing to greater literacy and the ability to express ideas. Parker explained art as a mode of expression to communicate ideas, and Mary Mann proposed that drawing enabled the expression of ideas and truths.

Exploring great ideas and truths was in vogue in educational circles as a general curricular emphasis, but the validity of those specific "great ideas" of others for modern day needs is debated. The "core curriculum" took a culture epoch or an immediate environmental concern as the common focus of several disciplines. Big ideas selected from writings of artists, dancers, poets, and writers become the focus in aesthetic education courses and in art curriculum development today.

Search for contemporary truths is basic in the social comment nature of much secondary level art in forms of collage, painting, drawing, prints, filmmaking, photography, aesthetics discussions, and happenings.

Others, sensitive to the contemporary scene, are seeking application of aesthetic truths in the total context in which humans exist. Interest in ecology; aesthetically ordering the environment; humanism; leisure; and social responsibility to the aesthetic context emerges. Art forms change as secondary students make meaningful statements about their concerns. These concerns are at least related to concerns formerly verbalized by others—Dow (space art), J. Ward Stinson (natural principles), and James Jackson (urban landscape).

Dealing with high level concepts demands a structure through which students can build. Whether breaking down the big idea or a general goal, art educators are finding a needed commitment to the learning process.

INDIVIDUALIZATION

Dewey and the Progressive Education movement stressed the individual, his society, and his values—emphases that were heralded by Victor D'Amico. Perhaps the moves toward valuing the individual student, along with pressure to be accountable for learning, have given impetus to the move to attend to the structure of learning in art. Student involvement in planning broadens learning activity options designed to develop concepts and competencies needed to meet objectives. Instructional materials centers and learning labs adapted to needs of the art student—perhaps incorporating the school-without-walls and open classroom ideas—allow art learning to encourage individual progression more officially than before. Recognition of the validity of an individual response and student-oriented teaching and planning (which many art teachers have advocated for years), is now being given support in general educational circles. Art teachers can find change in this direction compatible with their basic beliefs.

As one reviews even a sampling of trends in art education and considers current emphases, it becomes most obvious that any one bandwagon inadequately considers some other valid emphasis. Bandwagons usually call attention to some neglected aspect and so have their place. The temptation is to become so sold on a simplistic isolation of purpose, that art learning revolves around what the teacher wants to teach, rather than what students perceive as meaningful learning for their lives in a future world which we can only predict.

The art teacher must be aware of this danger, and then carefully select and synthesize the emphases appropriate both to his own time and to the students concerned.

REFERENCES

1　Michael Day, "Rationales for Art Education: Thinking Through and Telling Why," *Art Education*, Vol. 25, No. 2, February 1972, p. 18.
2　John Locke, *Some Thoughts Concerning Education*, Cambridge University Press, 1934, pp. 136-137, in Saunders, Robert J., "Selections from Historical Writings on Art Education," *Art Education*, Vol. 19, No. 1, January 1966, p. 26.
3　James S. Coleman, "Class Integration—A Fundamental Break with the Past," *Saturday Review*, Vol. IV, No. 22, May 27, 1972, p. 59.
4　Vincent Lanier, "Objectives of Teaching Art," *Art Education*, Vol. 25, No. 3, March 1972, p. 17.

Some Strategies for the Teaching of Art

Although there are many varied effective art programs in secondary schools across the nation, it is possible to determine several predominant approaches which are given emphasis in contemporary art education. Most art programs combine elements and emphases from several of these strategies; but some are rather heavily centered about one particular approach.

Many art programs are student-oriented, placing primary emphasis upon the needs of the particular group involved, recognizing their individual natures, their cultural, economic, and social backgrounds, and their potential for that humanistic growth which the arts can nurture.

The interdisciplinary program, on the other hand, focuses upon cultures—those values, meanings, and feelings of a civilization which are reflected in the art it produces, and which can then be related to contemporary society and its values. Such a program considers a civilization through several disciplines, generally the arts, philosophy, social studies, literature, math, and science.

In the stress upon the justification of art in the curriculum and upon accountability within the art program, behavioral objectives have gained considerable emphasis. This strategy attempts to structure the art program by establishing a set of goals in advance of instruction and then to design and implement the program toward achievement of the educational objectives.

The perceptual approach to art education stresses sensory awareness—the heightening of the individual's awareness of the world and of qualities within works of art.

Materials are made the basis for the experiential art program, in which students directly explore the qualities of art materials, discover possibilities for forming and expressing, and then create an art form consistent with the potentials and limitations of the particular material.

The frequent employment of an artist-in-residence in the schools in recent years has led to new emphasis upon the artist as a model for art education. In such an approach, students are encouraged to work in the manner of the professional, developing their ideas individually, setting their own projects, developing their own techniques, observing the methods of the professional artist and the works of artists of past and contemporary cultures, and evaluating their own work.

Recently art history has become a familiar part of the high school art curriculum in a number of schools across the nation. Such an emphasis upon art as a discipline is generally aimed at giving the student insight into works of art of varied styles of the past and the present, and enabling him to appreciate, understand, and form judgments about art objects from a wide range of cultures. Another possible emphasis of the high school art history program is enabling the student to fully commune with works of art in a direct attitude of full aesthetic experience.

There are other current emphases in art education: design principles; the study of art in relation to social problems; the formal study of art as a discipline; approaches to art through the media; and others.

There is, fortunately, no one way to teach art. Every teacher must find his own way. What he does depends upon what he is, and what he believes; it depends upon the particular group of students involved—their backgrounds, nature, and needs; it depends upon what the teacher knows and is able to use—in short, his preparation, experience, and the materials and facilities available; and it depends upon the philosophy of the school and the climate of the community.

But most of all, it depends upon what the teacher is, as an individual with sensitivity, compassion, and the capacity to experience aesthetically.[1] For no amount of materials and facilities, no amount of educational background, planning, or skill, can replace that indefinable quality by which a teacher reaches a student, that communion in the presence of experience, insights, and feelings, that sensitivity, respect, and caring, by which something deep and beautiful is led into being within the individual, and he is made finer and more human. To ignite this spark, and to keep it burning, is to teach.

REFERENCES

1 For further discussion of the art teacher's role in aesthetic education, see: "Aesthetic Education: An Education for the Immediacy of Sensuous Experience," Duke (W.J.) Madenfort, *Art Education*, May 1972, Washington, D.C.: The National Art Education Association. Vol. 25, No. 5, pp. 10-14.

The Student-Centered Approach

A student-centered art education program is based primarily upon each individual's cultural, psychological, and physical needs and interests, and upon his level of cognition, emotional reaction, and perceptual sensitivity.

Self-expression is an important element in the student-centered approach. The term, which was used considerably during the progressive education movement, has appeared in many publications in the field. Gradually as more was learned through research about the nature of children and adolescents, many art educators, including Viktor Lowenfeld, recommended recognition of stages of development and some degree of teacher structuring in order to offset negative attitudes about artistic activity and to further the growth of visual "creative" abilities in students.

The word "creative," although quite popular, was used in association with "self-expression" without a clear definition by some authors (Lowenfeld was one of those who tried to define the term—it is still largely undefined). Group methods of guiding students to express themselves in some personal way according to their feelings and visual perceptions, their imagery or symbols, was championed by Lowenfeld and many of his contemporaries. Certainly Lowenfeld was moving toward a more balanced approach between teacher dominated and complete student-centered *laissez-faire* views.

THE OPEN CLASSROOM

Americans have been hearing much about the open classroom approach that is being imported mainly from Great Britain. In this type of program, students are encouraged to plan their own curriculum and to choose their subjects for study. Teachers share in discoveries, set up learning environments, and make materials for learning available. Student plans are discussed, and the teachers may ask challenging questions or let students continue without much guidance. The emphasis of the open classroom appears to be upon the satisfaction of psychological needs for self-identity, self-motivation, and self-confidence. This is a direct contrast to individualized programmed learning, and other variations of the neo-academic approach, which leaves all concern for the "self" to the parents.

Some art educators are reshaping their art programs into the new academic framework that has been developed by their school districts. A danger in all of this structuring is the possibility that studio learning (with innovative self-discovery) may be dropped from the art program. Another equally grave danger is that in the concentration upon conceptual, academic knowledge in art, the direct experiencing of a work of art may be neglected or denied, and that no allowance will be made for development of the individual's capacity for sensuous, aesthetic experience, either of nature or of the work of art.

The old and outdated idea that only the gifted will become artists and therefore that only they should receive studio education is being raised from apparent oblivion, and used again in some instances in order to justify removing studio learning from art programs for the majority of students. Art educators who feel forced to develop more teacher-dominated, structured art programs in the secondary schools have the difficult task of seeing that they do not structure the aesthetic experience out of art, and students out of the art program.

Some educators believe that the student-centered approach leaves too much permissiveness in the art classroom, but such a program need not mean an extreme of freedom to do as one pleases. There can be a student-centered, but sensitively directed approach.

THE STUDENT-CENTERED IN-DEPTH APPROACH

Beyond the dichotomy of teacher-dominated, structured programs and student centered, permissive programs, is another way which stresses neither academic rules and concepts nor complete freedom for the student. This third approach is student-centered in that it focuses upon the visual, artistic being of each individual student; at the same time the teacher has an active role to play, too. Each student is challenged by the teacher toward self-evaluation of his art products in order to 1) observe his own personal art expressions during the process of formation and upon completion; 2) record positive and negative aspects contained in these expressed art forms; 3) analyze the nature of any visual successes or problems; 4) solve problems in terms of the chosen art media; 5) relate solutions to similar solutions found in the art works of others of past and present—relate to certain historical art works, for example; 6) learn concepts and skills as these relate to personal levels of achievement, and 7) share process and product problems and solutions with others.

This student-centered approach involves a teacher-directed self-guidance method and recognizes the possibility of the inherent synthesizing power of artistic vision in the human psyche. It is student-centered in so far as the art process comes from a center deep within the student's being. Insofar as it is directed by a teacher through particular questioning techniques, it may also be termed teacher-dominated. A teacher-guide is needed to help students to reach beyond the enculturated outer layers of their minds in order to contact again their powers of visual conceiving, sensuous experience, and artistic cognition.

Other approaches such as giving high school students individual "turfs" or studios, letting them come and go when they please, setting up programmed work stations, and so on, can be handled meaningfully within this approach. In a student-centered approach of this kind, humanism is the touch stone. The aim is to help the individual realize the fullest measure of the light of artistic vision within him.

Interdisciplinary Studies

Interdisciplinary studies, team teaching, multi-media, inter-media, humanities, and aesthetic education are all terms that indicate an opening up of the traditional pigeon-holed subject matter and self-contained classroom, even though each of the terms is open to numerous definitions and approaches. Each recognizes that education is ultimately as big as life and must be integrated from various sources and disciplines, and each embodies a complexity of elements within a unified statement.

Theoreticians and purists isolate learning and identify with labels of academia and then establish academic imperatives for studying such minutiae. Such specialties undoubtedly have their meaningful place. To effectively integrate knowledge and experience one must also perceive the singular nature of each area. The experience of a good meal, for instance, is to experience each exquisite taste sensation that is part of that meal; and to be aware of the environment, the service, sound, company, et al, that add up to the single "meal" experience, which in turn is related to one's total being. Specific understandings should always precede generalizations, or there is danger of superficiality. But the proliferation of courses and demands on student time, the common fragmentation of student and teacher experience, and over-specialization at the high school level have given us reason for re-thinking curriculum and the interdisciplinary possibilities.

An approach utilizing varied disciplines may not necessarily be an interdisciplinary approach. Humanities, for instance, may actually present single concept teaching of several disciplines rather than an interrelated approach. Even with four team members, each may just be presenting his subject specialty with only a new name and scheduling format but with their old inviolate solo classroom approach. In this situation, hopefully an infrequent one, interdisciplinary stresses may just lessen the effectiveness of a good "traditional" teacher.

In some instances the interdisciplinary approach may be instituted better by one teacher than by a team or a group. The teacher might find needed expertise through volunteer and community resources, or in open communication with like-minded staff members. Students also may have numerous contributions or talents to offer in establishing an interdisciplinary ambiance.

As an example of an interdisciplinary program, we will consider one midwestern high school which established a Fine Arts Department combining drama, art, music, humanities, film and dance. The department also administered extra-curricular arts activities. Department coordination encouraged interdisciplinary approaches, although they were not mandated. Existing personnel interests and background determined somewhat the extent of the program, and as new staff additions were made, new stresses were brought into the program, for example the addition of a dance-drama combination major to the faculty. Some of the subjects were specialized, such as acting, art foundations, chorus, orchestra, and band, but many others had interrelated approaches.

Another aspect of this approach was an experimental program for "alienated" students, emphasizing alternatives to education. In this program, students were encouraged to initiate interdisciplinary projects as well as traditional ones, with assistance from assigned teachers or outside resources. Their interests were varied and sometimes quite traditional. Teacher-initiated programs were minimized to allow student direction to emerge and to encourage cooperative student-teacher curriculum development. Four subject area teachers were assigned to approximately 60 students without prescribed class periods. This program provided more flexible student-teacher relationships and subject-area exploration.

Workshops or mini-courses were created to replace the traditional clubs, and to stimulate new ideas and to service varied student needs. An example was the Photography Club, which had consisted of a relatively static group which met erratically throughout the year. It was supplanted by a six-week workshop, a mini-course without prerequisites or credit, with lectures by outside professionals. The group travelled to a nearby university for an intensive week-end workshop in photo-techniques, as well as human relations explorations related to photography. The photography study offered professional level instruction open to all interested students at all levels in the school.

Another special feature was an experimental workshop led by a young kinetic-electronics artist. This workshop not only proved exciting to a group of art-oriented students, but attracted two sophomore electronics "experts" who found a new avenue for their interests and became deeply involved in this form of expression.

Open labs were set up in the school, so that students could come to work with available art teachers during unscheduled periods and where they could get assistance and could have access to special equipment. Special-purpose art rooms helped provide for this added opportunity for individual work. Open labs can be especially effective when students have learned to motivate their own independent directions, and open labs in turn can help develop the capacity for independent work.

At this particular high school, filmmaking was not a formal course, and it often involved an interested student, an optional class project, and the expertise of various faculty: the art teacher, audiovisual specialist, the film study teacher, and the classroom teacher. This type of cooperation exists frequently in many schools and is perhaps typical of the interdisciplinary basic approach and recognition of attempts to integrate student experience despite formalized subject lines and fragmented class assignments.

The humanities team combined art, English, social studies, and music, utilizing small and large group presentations, guest lecturers, outside resources, and studio experiences in each of the subject areas. Independent study projects, required at the end of the semester, utilized the interdisciplinary approach or the more traditional research type of project, depending on student interest.

A musical-comedy production brought experts from varied disciplines—music personnel, art direction, tech crews, drama personnel, and dancers, into a dramatic unity. This traditional theatre form is an effective way to demonstrate interdisciplinary approaches although it doesn't often reach the "Total Theatre" concept envisioned as far back as Richard Wagner or the Bauhaus, or as currently as Alwin Nikolais' Dance Theatre. Rock operas and multi-media productions can add new dimensions to traditional theatre offerings and can be one more step towards the ideal of the interdisciplinary or total theatre concept. Each aspect of a "Total Theatre" production should be vital in itself and not just an ancillary to major dramatic action. Just as Sir Wilfred's "Lumia" became a concert without sound, not just light to illuminate a stage, film also might be used as a major "character" rather than just a supporting technique for the scene designer. Some intermedia pieces present a poem read with musical accompaniment and/or slide projections. Even such a minor experiment can be enough to awaken the potential of the interdisciplinary giant: the multi-media production. Art students and teachers built a "Kaleidoscope," utilizing a large mirror box with fabric backdrop receiving projected images. Students danced and moved behind this sheet to create abstract shadow patterns with the accompaniment of musicians or records. The combination of images was reflected infinitely in an engrossing multi-faceted arts experience.

Interdisciplinary developments depend primarily on the teacher. Such an approach cannot be just a routine assignment. A teacher is his own best textbook. If he is actually engaged in the interdisciplinary approach and dedicated to its basic truth, he will lead his students towards that end. If, for example, he requires electrical assistance to activate his sculpture in a desired new direction, he will learn those principles wherever he can and engender in his students that sense of search and respect for other skills. If one is studying rituals, he undoubtedly will seek the dancers, the singers, the artists, the actors (as they might exist within his given group of students) who will help him create a meaningful and total type of statement, and who will motivate his students to join him in his search or will start them on their own when relevant. A summer workshop would be invaluable in teaching personnel as well as students how to work with related disciplines and staff and to concretize new possibilities in school structure and attitudes.

A school curriculum is by nature limited. Though a student might want specialized instruction in all disciplines, he is constrained by time. It is desirable to study each art form individually, but it might be even more practical to introduce them in one aesthetic education survey where the essential elements of dance, art, music, and drama can be studied with or without studio participation. Proliferation of courses, demands on student time, and fragmented efforts lead to new evaluations of basic concepts needed for high school education. One art can relate to any other art form or to any other subject. One must keep in mind the distinctive flavors of each as well as the interrelatedness of all. The artist-in-residence program at the high school under discussion included an interdisciplinary sculpture workshop, which reached out to other related skills and knowledge—from the English class studying mythology to the auto workshop. Students had no formal time commitment or grades, and the atmosphere encouraged each person to bring all of himself to his work, contributing whatever skills and interests he had. Other faculty visited the studio and had easy exchanges with the teacher and students, which fomented interchanges of ideas. Formalizing such a creative interdisciplinary approach demands careful philosophical preparation, not just a label and a time slot.

The high school project "Focus on the Arts" represented an additional extra curricular opportunity for students to experience a multiplicity of art forms as both audience and presenter. The professions and the community participated in an intensive encounter-week of art, drama, music, film, creative writing, and photography. It was sponsored by the Fine Arts Department and paid for by the PTA. Innumerable new interests and potential students emerged from the stimuli of the week.

"Star Series," ten non-required lecture/presentations held throughout the school year, presented practicing artists and performers to an enthusiastic student audience. By the time a student had attended four years of available Star Series and Focus programs, plus available art shows, open workshops, labs, and plays, the arts curriculum had been extended to an entire student body. The formal arts enrollment, perhaps because of this additional impetus, far exceeded the usual anticipated numbers in the typical suburban college-oriented high school.

The humanities program is an especially popular interdisciplinary approach. It stresses an examination of varied cultures as reflections of man's values, attitudes, and beliefs, approaching the study through a number of disciplines. One high school in the Midwest designed a humanities program known as "The Human Enterprise"—a special course for juniors and seniors interested in an interdisciplinary approach involving art, music, literature, and history. Instructional staff consisted of three teachers, representing literature, philosophy, and art, with frequent guest speakers, field trips, group discussions, and visual presentations included in the curriculum. Students received one unit of credit for the year, with a credit/no credit option.

The program was originated by a small group of high school faculty who mutually arrived at the conclusion that the school should develop a humanities program. The school administration approved, and a committee met for one year, all departments represented, to collect and discuss materials that might be relevant to the new course. At the end of this exploratory year, the scope of the program had been defined and a tentative teaching team had been organized. This humanities team then spent a second year in detailed planning of the curriculum; class activity started the third year. Although many changes were made, much of the original direction and philosophy of the planning years was retained.

The following were part of the basic structure of the program:

1) The program was interdisciplinary in the sense that it was not attached to any other department for administrative purposes.
2) A separate budget was maintained for supplies, equipment, and staff travel.
3) The curriculum was idea-centered rather than traditional and chronological.
4) Curriculum and job assignments were a mutually shared responsibility.
5) Students were motivated to be active participants in program activities, frequently involved in planning and performing their own curricula.

The content course revolved around three basic ideas: "The Search for Beliefs and Values," "The Glory of Secular Life," and "Man and His Relationship to Man." Curricular emphasis altered from year to year to accommodate changes in staff, and student interests. Presentation of material remained innovative, with a format which invited student participation.

A brief handbook was produced yearly to contain materials for reference throughout the year, including a statement of course goals, overview of the curriculum, course requirements, mode of operation, and basic reference materials related to the disciplines which structured the course. The publication became a standard of mechanical operation.

The basic philosophy of the course is expressed in the following:

> Man, a social animal, is born from the cumulative experience of culture. He is constantly influenced by the diffusion of experiences from the past, which he uses as a guide and as a source of inspiration for the present and future. He uses the arts as an expression of his individual values, problems, and feelings; but he and his arts cannot exist alone. He lives in a social context with other men, searching with them for the love, peace, and understanding that have always been the goals of the Human Enterprise.

The course focused on the questions: "Who am I? Why am I? Where am I going?" By reflection and action, students were led to:

1) Develop an awareness of the life of the mind;

2) Examine literature, history, philosophy, music, and art as man's expression of his experiences, ideas, and values;
3) Become not only intelligent but also compassionate human beings;
4) Attempt to improve the balance between materialistic values and ethical values by becoming involved in knowledge and experiences which can help develop a social conscience.

Major strengths of the humanities program at this particular school were found to be the following:

1) A strong and well trained staff who were willing to meet often, to take one another's suggestions, to endure the pressures of team teaching, and to relate their own disciplines to the larger whole of the humanities.
2) A well-developed course of study, concise and detailed, which still allowed for shifts of emphasis and teaching materials.
3) The option of taking the course for credit rather than the traditional letter grade.
4) An administration that both encouraged and supported the program.
5) A "live" format which included frequent guest speakers, field trips, and audiovisual materials.
6) A curriculum that included student participation at several levels, including two functioning committees—a curriculum and an evaluation committee, as well as planned student action in class.
7) An adequate budget for the purchase of equipment and supplies.
8) A librarian acting as a resource consultant for both students and staff.
9) A greater flexibility of operation, with class scheduled for the last two periods of the day, excellent for field trips.

Major weaknesses of the program were the following:

1) Communication with students
   a. Projecting good oral communication with a large (75) group of students.
   b. Fostering adequate dialogue between individual students and staff members.
   c. Guarding against loss of individual student identity.
   d. Motivating adequate self-discipline and mature judgment.
2) Communication with staff
   a. Lack of sufficent time for class preparation on the part of the humanities team, who had additional responsibilities in other teaching and administrative assignments.
3) Physical facilities
   a. With a total course enrollment of 150, the crowded class and space conditions seriously hindered sight and hearing of lectures and general communication.

The greatest single indicator of effectiveness was student-parent reaction to the program. Students liked the course, talked to fellow students about the content, and encouraged them to enroll in the program. Graduated seniors visiting the school indicated how well the course had prepared them for college work, both through program content and individual discipline. Parents indicated that their children were more interested in discussing ideas as a result of the course.

The measure of success of the humanities program was attributed largely to the nature of the ideas which were the focal points of the course: the questions of the nature of man and his relationship to the world around him. The student confronted these questions through varied disciplines in an integrated manner —an approach strikingly different from any other experience in his school life. While he did not always find solutions to his own problems, the quest itself was often a source of deep satisfaction.

There are endless variations in the possible content, approaches, emphases, and structure of interdisciplinary programs. They offer a unique way to discover similarities and differences in the various arts and humanities, to relate man to his culture, and to become involved with man's search for meaning and values. The arts are the logical leaders in interdisciplinary studies, because they can and do relate to all aspects of living and learning, and they involve the whole person, cognitively and affectively, fusing the intellectual, the emotional, and the sensuous as a way of knowing.

Art Approached Behaviorally

The behavioral approach to art education is a point of view held by those who believe that student behavior can be altered as a result of educational experience. Planning of art experiences related to real life situations becomes a tool to make possible more effective learning oriented toward life objectives. Fundamental to this approach is the discipline of setting attainable goals, establishing priorities, applying methods of research to on-going instructional tasks, and developing tools for assessment and evaluation.

A major problem in establishing behaviorally based art curricula has been the scope of the problem. What art behaviors are desirable and relevant? How can one go about achieving these behaviors? How can he assess the extent to which goals are being realized? Can he identify what can be learned, what will be taught, what kinds of student behavior will be altered?

In the 60's, recognition of the need for the American educational system to make severe breaks with traditional practices brought about such innovations as programmed instruction, large group instruction, team teaching, individually guided instruction, unitized schools, and flexible modular scheduling—to name but a few of the many organizational patterns. These changes were attempts to meet the needs of students in a rapidly changing world. It was thought that changed organization might facilitate the aim of leading students to comprehension of concepts instead of mastery of verbal information.

Changed organizational patterns did not necessarily bring innovations in curriculum and teaching methodology, particularly as related to development of specific, attainable goals. Nor did test results in academic areas indicate higher student scores.

A growing public cry for accountability gave impetus to behaviorally based curriculum efforts in many areas of study. In the visual arts curriculum development was given support by numerous grants from private foundations as well as the federal government. Colleges and universities organized federally and privately funded seminars and workshops. Grants to local schools and state departments of public instruction made possible curriculum development on local and state levels.

The greatest impetus to the behavioral objectives approach to art education was provided by the federally funded NAEA Preconference Seminars held in various parts of the country in 1968, 1969, and 1970. These seminars brought together art educators at all levels of the profession for serious study of curriculum development. Led by Asahel D. Woodruff, the seminars challenged participants to take a new look at goals, practices, and outcomes of art education.

The NAEA Research Seminars contributed to clarification of three major aspects of curriculum planning based on expected behavior: 1) establishment of precise, attainable goals; (2) identification of behaviors; (3) development of assessment and evaluative techniques.

GOALS

In early sessions of the 1968 Conference, goals as traditionally stated were torn apart. The search for precise, attainable objectives made participants increasingly aware of the need for greater specificity in statement of goals and a consequent restructuring of curriculum based on real life situations of students.

The precise assumptions on which Barkan and Chapman had developed goals for *TV Guidelines in Art*[1] were of considerable importance in establishing goals for behaviorally based art curricula. The assumptions, based on the interrelated aspects of making, perceiving, and understanding, provided a basis for planning broadly based art experiences capable of affecting behavior.

Behaviorally based art curricula stand on the premise that student behavior can be changed through experiences in these three areas: (1) Learning to make art; (2) Learning to perceive, to see, and to feel; and (3) Learning to understand art. Acceptance of these three areas of experience as goals implies interrelationships. Planning must be broad and inclusive if behavior is to be affected. Daily tasks are stated in behavioral terms, and daily learnings fit into the total.

Acceptance of these three types of experience is recognition that many types of behaviors contribute to reaching the goals.

ART BEHAVIORS

Behavioral objectives proponents early recognized the need for study and categorization of art behaviors. Participants in the 1969 NAEA Seminars formulated carrier tasks, analyzed competencies necessary to the performance of these tasks, and worked out tables of specifications. Work on these problems reaffirmed the recognition that curriculum development in art based on behavioral outcomes was dependent upon identification of behavior relevant for education in art.

Donald Jack Davis[2] reviewed and synthesized various types of behavior that make up real life situations and came up with this summary outline of seven commonly accepted types:

1. Perception Behaviors
    a. Viewing - looking at - seeing and recognizing the environment

    b. Viewing - looking at - seeing and recognizing works of art

    c. Developing awareness - receiving

2. Knowing Behaviors
   a. Understanding the language of art
   b. Understanding about artists and their works

3. Reacting Behaviors
   a. Experience
   b. Feeling

4. Analytical Behaviors
   a. Classifying
   b. Describing
   c. Explaining
   d. Interpreting

5. Judgment and Evaluation Behaviors
   a. Criticizing
   b. Estimating

6. Execution Behaviors
   a. Developing creativity - fluency, flexibility, originality and the like
   b. Synthesizing
   c. Learning to use tools and materials
   d. Making, doing, producing art forms

7. Valuing Behaviors - attitudes

As this summary suggests, the diverse nature of art experiences forces art educators to be concerned with behaviors in the cognitive, affective, and motor-skill domains. Varied kinds of experiences provide the vehicle for effecting change in student behavior.

EVALUATION AND ASSESSMENT

Identification of goals and types of learning are necessary steps to the development of assessment instruments. Public pleas for accountability in all areas of education focused attention on assessment and evaluation in art. What proof can be given that art instruction is affecting student behavior?

The varied types of art behaviors inherent in *learning to make art, learning to see and feel,* and *learning to understand art,* make obvious the need for different kinds of assessment and evaluative techniques. While art educators have been slow in developing tools for evaluation and assessment, considerable progress has been made. One thing is certain: there is an increasing awareness of the need for valid instruments.

Inclusion of the visual arts in National Assessment led to development of behaviorally based assessment items under the direction of Brent Wilson, Special Consultant to National Assessment. Wilson's review of the literature on

"Evaluation of Learning in Art Education"[3] summarizes seven types of testing procedures:

Testing for Perception	Testing for Evaluation
Testing for Knowledge	Testing for Appreciation
Testing for Comprehension	Testing for Production
Testing for Analysis	Formative Evaluation

Art educators who hold to behaviorally based art programs would agree that all types of testing procedures are necessary if we are to assess types of behavior and the extent to which we are meeting the goals of *learning to make art, learning to see and feel,* and *learning to understand art.*

The behavioral approach to art education focuses attention on the need for art instruction based on life experiences as a means of changing behavior. Thoughtfully developed behaviorally based art curricula may well be the solution to our challenge of accountability.

With the whole trend of education moving toward more and more accountability, our instructional programs in the arts must show evidence that we are effecting changes in art behaviors. To attain our rightful image and proper place in the educational complex, these changes must speak clearly of the need for art instruction for all individuals.[4]

REFERENCES

1 Manuel Barkan, and Laura Chapman, *Guidelines for Art Instruction through Television for Elementary Schools,* Unpublished 4th Draft 1967.
2 Donald Jack Davis, "Human Behavior: Its Implications for Curriculum Development in Art," *Studies in Art Education,* NAEA, Volume 12, Number 3, Spring 1971, pp. 3-12.
3 Benjamin S. Bloom, J. Thomas Hastings, and George Madaus,: *Handbook on Formative and Summative Evaluation of Student Learning.* New York: McGraw Hill Book Company, 1971.
  Wilson, Brent G., Chapter 17, Part 2, "Evaluation of Learning in Art Education," pp. 530-553.
4 Donald Jack Davis, *ibid,* p. 7.

Art Approached as Perception

All art education is concerned with perception—with knowing, feeling, and expressing through sensory awareness. Some art programs place primary emphasis upon perception.

> *Sensory perception, the key to acquiring of all knowledges, is a basic phenomenal act. It is far from being a process of mere recording of sensory elements, nor is it the impassive registering of shapes, colors, and sounds. Rather, the process of sensory perception is an active and selective exploration of the world around us.*[1]

This concept has not always been understood. Rudolf Arnheim informs us that it is "only recent psychological thinking that encourages us to call vision a creative activity of the human mind."[2] This opinion is supported by Gyorgy Kepes in his book, *Language of Vision,* "To perceive a visual image implies the beholder's participation in a process of organization. The experience of an image is thus a creative act of integration."[3]

So that perception is not just interpreted within its present framework, a look into the past will reveal much divergent thinking about why man viewed each society as he did. In studying this concept through the eyes of historians, one might come to believe that as many theories exist as do historians. Yet in spite of the fact that theories differ, the statement that man was a sensitive, perceptive being as far back as 17,000 years ago is evident. The early cave paintings in France testify to this. No matter whether these early motivations to paint stemmed from magical or spiritual impulses or the desire to express what was seen, the rich, earthy representations of animal forms, exquisite examples of sensitive perception have been left for all to witness. Primitive man saw; he felt; he responded to the world about him in a unique way that had meaning for him.

Each group of men that followed left a visual trail, the result of their particular manner of perception. Gyorgy Kepes says:

> *In each age of human history man was compelled to search for a temporary equilibrium in his conflicts with nature and his relationship to other men, and thus created, through an organization of visual imagery, a symbolic order of his psychological and intellectual experience. These forms of his creative imagination directed him and inspired him toward materializing the potential order inherent in each stage of history.*[4]

Perception should be given special attention within existing art curricula. Some secondary schools and many colleges have semester courses devoted to the area. While it is true that man sees mainly to fill his needs, and that he sees what he wants to see, perception is a gift given to all in some degree, and the sensuous visual experience and level of awareness involved are essential to man as a human individual.

A program in perception should help students develop, recognize, and participate in sensations with intensity and sensitivity and should broaden their sensory scope. Such a concentrated program could produce permanent change in the level of the student's awareness.

Rudolf Arnheim has attempted to isolate the experience of perception and to study it from a scientific, psychological standpoint. In his *Art and Visual Perception,* he deals with the visual image from the point of view of gestalt psychology, viewing a whole image in relation to its parts.

A simple statement of the learning process might be: a stimulus, a sensation, perception, choice. A given stimulus creates a sensation within us; it is realized in the mind to form a perception, and it leaves us then open to choices. A person may integrate the knowledge and make it a part of himself; he may totally reject it; he may keep the result of such perception completely to himself; he may transform the perception into an expression; or he may find that some of the experiences take on a distorted view due to past associations.[5]

The following statement by June King McFee synthesizes thoughts on perception as they become meaningful in an art program:

> *The emphasis made on the need for perceptual training of children and students may cause some cries of "If you do this, you will stifle creativity. Artists today do not just copy nature." This criticism usually comes from people that are not aware of the complexity of the visual process. Visual training increases the wealth of material children have to work with. If visual training becomes rigid and authoritarian, it may inhibit creative activity; but if used to motivate visual curiosity and exploration, it should widen the range of creative instruction.*[6]

An example of a high school art program largely based upon perception is that of one large suburban school which offers a semester course in *Perception,* providing experiences in exploring the visual, tactile, auditory, olfactory, and taste senses. During the course, students build tactile walls which they then experience through touching with their eyes closed. Explorations take place outdoors, also, where blindfolded and led by a friend, students discover bricks, grass, trees, and other forms and surfaces with a new insight and enthusiasm. Auditory investigations cover every range of sound, including creative tapes of sounds; the excitement of orchestrating 24 transistor radios; and documenting a five-mile automobile ride as a blindfolded passenger, recording a trail of sounds. Enjoying cooking tastes and fragrances, together with other students, is another aspect of the course.

The art program based upon perception hopefully leads to increased sensuous awareness, and a greater sensitivity to and involvement in aesthetic experiences, both in the environment and in works of art. As modern society offers man more and more leisure time, facing him with the possibility of richly enjoyable free time, or boredom and destructive pursuits, it is especially imperative that the individual learn to experience sensuously and aesthetically, to derive meaning and pleasure from the world around him, and from the realm of the arts. The art program based upon perception and sensuous awareness hopes to educate man for a more aesthetic and meaningful life.

REFERENCES

1 Hazel Loew, *Planned Perception in the Art Program,* thesis, Illinois Institute of Technology, Chicago, Illinois, 1966, p. 1.
2 Rudolf Arnheim, *Art and Visual Perception,* 3rd. Berkeley and Los Angeles: University of California Press, 1960, p. 31.
3 Gyorgy Kepes, *Language of Vision,* 1st ed. Chicago: Paul Theobold, 1944, p. 13.
4 *Ibid.,* p. 14.
5 Robert Roth, I.I.T., July 1964. Notes taken from lecture in course "Fundamentals in Counseling and Psychotherapy."
6 June King McFee, *Preparation for Art.* San Francisco: Wadsworth Publishing Co., 1961, p. 38.

Art Approached
Experientially

Some art programs are based largely upon explorations with materials. The student is guided to discover the qualities of a variety of art materials, to evolve forms and ideas from them, and to develop an art expression in a manner consistent with the nature and limitations of the material. Such an approach is largely experiential, since the student's awareness and responsiveness and the forms he develops, are based upon his experience as he works directly in the particular material.

The wide range of materials available today for classroom use stand as both an opportunity and a threat to educational goals. As simply an "experience" in wood block printing, ceramics, or papier maché, the experiential approach can reduce art to a disconnected sequence of activities. ("We've *had* block printing.") As "projects," it can become a teacher-directed "do-it-yourself-kit" requiring only obedience to directions.

In the face of mounting drop-out statistics and increasing criticism of the education system, these goals are being reassessed. Formative rather than factual goals are finding recognition. Art educators must realize that this is their hour. Art can become, in Herbert Read's words, the "mode of education," the visual approach to the entire educational process. And the materials' potential is an important factor, provided it is used with growth rather than product objectives.

A review of these growth objectives will clarify this position.

The experiential approach should expand the student's aesthetic awareness, his perception. The importance of this to the person and therefore its role as a major educational goal becomes ever more evident in a society which tends toward increased passivity and control in work and recreational situations. Awareness is essential to preserve the very humanity of the individual.

The experiential approach should challenge the student to explore, to make creative, *risk* decisions. Too much learning is programmed to a predetermined outcome. An experiential approach to materials offers the child the challenge to discover the possibilities of a material, to respect its limits, to work with its nature. It is essential, in presenting these materials, that they not be narrowed into a teacher-planned object. The child must learn to think with the material, to make a decision and follow it through. Planning an approach, seeking information and materials, and solving intermediate steps are all invaluable learning skills that art can teach the child.

A program based on materials should foster in the student the ability to cope with failure. In a fact-oriented educational system measured by testing, failure has only one connotation. Learning through creative risk-taking must allow for a positive view of failure as a step toward deeper discovery. An experiential approach to art structures just such a learning situation. An unsatisfactory result creates the moment of teacher-student assessment of material, skill, design quality that is basic to real learning. The opportunity to rethink and act upon such evaluation must be allowed for.

Related to these goals of risk-taking and building on failure is the social value of such a classroom atmosphere. Success must not be seen as doing better than others but rather as achieving one's own goals. Critiques of works done in this climate can be open, unembarrassing, and enlightening. Group participation in solving problems arising from exploring a new material can create a peer-relationship free of inhibition and fear of humiliation.

The experiential approach should develop understanding of form through a variety of materials. Form and expression as well as the material itself should be the lead-in to presentation of a new material. Materials can be introduced in relation to *search* for line quality, 3-D shape, etc. The properties of materials determine the form resulting. Actual handling of many materials is important to give the student a first-hand experience of the palette knife versus the bristle versus the wash brush, or the textures achieved with terra cotta clay, papier maché, wood carving, and plaster.[1]

Line can be approached by gathering together as many tools as possible for making lines: sticks, cardboard edges, straws, sponges, as well as pen points, chalk, crayons, and brushes. Qualities of lines—thickness, smoothness, texture, etc., can be explored by students and compared and used to express ideas such as power, weakness, confusion. Widely varied works of art should be presented for comparison of line qualities. Students then may approach their own work, making their own decisions about tools, ideas, approach, and expression.

Wood or linoleum block printing and etching can be presented as linear media, explored for the kinds of line that their tools can make. Other printing approaches—glue prints, cardboard, and string, can be tried and perfected, each for its own *form* potential. Approached in this way, materials offer a constant challenge to search and decision-making. No formula for outcome should be presented. Techniques for handling the materials—wedging clay, hollowing clay forms for firing, etc. should be taught within the search for the properties of the material.

Three-dimensional form should be approached through exploration of the varied potentials of materials and the varied approaches they require. The lightness and openness of form achieved with wire sculpture, the potential of balance it affords, the building-up process it entails, can be compared to the heaviness and solidity of a plaster-vermiculite carved form, the base balance, the cutting away process. And these can be seen as differing in form and expressive potential from papier maché, balsa or toothpick construction, ceramic modeling, or ceramic slab construction, macramé, and weaving.

Experiential art education can extend such understanding of form and material to encompass the materials of architecture and engineering. Sensitivity to materials developed through these simple materials of art will prepare the student to understand the still construction, reinforced concrete, geodesic dome structure, fiberglass, or plastics of today's world from their form potential and to approach architecture employing these, with sensitivity. Comparison of these to the wood and stone structures of the past develops understanding of honesty in use of materials, forms possible in each, and functions that each type adapts to.

Contemporary materials should be included in today's art curriculum. Light media—slides, overhead projections, forms involving light tubes or bulbs wired and even programmed offer new challenges to creative thinking.

Sound media can be incorporated in multi-media problems with tape recorders and with instruments designed and made.

Kinetic form opens whole new material possibilities including the electrical. Kinetic form should begin with the potential of the body for movement and form. Dancing, shape design in jersey sacks are dynamic approaches to 3-D form in sculpture.

Photography, motion picture, and even closed circuit television are accessible today for classroom use and offer their own extension of the students' understanding of form.[2]

All of the above objectives pertain to the development of skills and understandings. The importance of the experiential approach is stated by Jerome Bruner in *The Process of Education:*

> *Mastering of the fundamental ideas of a field involves not only the grasping of general principles but also the development of an attitude toward learning and inquiry, toward guessing and hunches, toward the possibility of solving problems on one's own . . .*[3]

Bruner goes on to point out that the important ingredient is the sense of excitement about discovery, discovery of previously unrecognized relations, similarities between ideas, with a resulting sense of self-confidence in one's abilities.

John Dewey, in *Education and Experience,* warns about the danger of experience isolated and over-directed.

> *Experience and education cannot be directly equated to each other. For some experiences are mis-educative. Any experience is mis-educative*

that has the effect of arresting or distorting the growth of further experience. An experience may be such as to engender callousness. It may produce lack of sensitivity and of responsiveness . . . Again, a given experience may increase a person's automatic skill in a particular direction and yet tend to land him in a groove or rut; the effect again is to narrow the field of further experience.[4]

He continues, pointing to the possibility of experiences being enjoyable but productive of carelessness; or of their being disconnected and therefore hindering future control. Experience, he says, should arouse curiosity, strengthen initiative, and set up desires and purposes intense enough to carry over dead places in the future.

The principles, according to Dewey, are continuity and interaction, the longitudinal and lateral aspects of education.

In conclusion, in a culture such as the present, where there is so much pressure toward uniformity of taste in our mass media of communication, so much passivity in work and entertainment, it is essential that the child be given confidence in his intuition, courage to follow it, and the desire to keep expanding his understanding.

REFERENCES
1 Jean Mary Mormon, *Art: of Wonder and a World.* Blauvelt, N. Y.: Art Education, Inc., 1967.
2 Jean Mary Mormon, *Art: Tempo of Today.* Blauvelt, N.Y.: Art Education, Inc. 1969.
3 Jerome Bruner, *The Process of Education.* Cambridge: Harvard University Press, 1960, p. 20.
4 John Dewey, *Education and Experience.* New York: Macmillan Company, 1938, p. 13.

The Artist as Model

In an effort to make the art experiences of students as relevant and meaningful as possible, some art educators base their programs upon the artist as a model for student art activity. The rationale for such a strategy is the need to involve students in the arts, to provide a program which instead of being remote—a study *about* works of art, artists, techniques, and styles—brings the student into direct contact with the artist as a human being and a professional.

In this approach to art instruction, the student can get to really know a professional artist. He can observe the artist at work, discuss ideas with him, and take him as a kind of model, so that the student, through the association, can learn to work in a more independent, relevant manner, developing his own ideas, learning to criticize his own work as it progresses, largely directing himself, and evaluating his own growth.

The artist-in-residence program in schools across the nation—a program which has spread widely in recent years, offers an effective means to this strategy, since the artist is employed for a considerable period of time, to work in a studio in or adjacent to the school, to participate and lead classroom activity in art, and to visit and discuss with students individually. Schools which do not have an artist-in-residence can still provide much first-hand experience with professionals, by inviting local artists to the classroom for lectures, discussion, and demonstrations, and by arranging for visits to the studios of local artists. Most communities have professional artists who will gladly come to the school as a guest speaker, to talk about their work and give demonstrations of their development of an art expression. It is the role of the art teacher to explore such possible resources within the community and in nearby communities.

Direct contact with a professional artist can have a significant impact upon high school students, giving them association with someone who is deeply involved with ideas and feelings and who is highly individual and responsive, with whom they can identify and share ideas. By contact with the artist, the student can learn what an artist is: a person who possesses a continuing sense of wonder and curiosity and at the same time has a high level of maturity by which he can make selective responses, organize them, and embody them in an art form; a person with a special sensuous awareness, who can experience aesthetically; a man who devotes his life to observing, sensing, and feeling, who searches, discovers, synthesizes, and creates anew; a man with technical skill, enthusiasm for hard work, and self-discipline, who is at the same time deeply sensitive. In getting to know the artist as a man, the high school student can gain valuable insight into the artistic nature which is a part, however latent, of every human being.

The artist-in-residence at a school should be made available to students for as much time as possible. There should be many opportunities for individual students to observe the artist at his work, to talk with him, and to watch the forming, clarification, self-criticism, and development of his work. There should be time for students to bring their own work to the artist for discussion—and times just for leisurely exchange of experiences and insights, so that students may get to know the artist as a person.

In getting to know the artist's way of life, the student should be inspired to broaden his own aesthetic experiences, to try new approaches in his own art expressions, to explore, feel, and express anew. The art teacher can help guide students into new ways of working which evolve from the experience with the professional artist and still permit the self-direction of the student.

The sensitive art teacher must know when to let the student proceed on his own, and when to direct, pointing out avenues of possibilities, and perhaps setting assignments. Having worked with the artist, a student might sometimes, like him, deliberately explore new approaches; for example he might develop a series of drawings in color, relating unrelated categories: vehicles and days of the week; shoes and electricity; vegetables and sound. A student might be directed to make color studies of a tomato and analysis of notes played by a guitar. Then he might combine the two, discovering new relationships. He might decide to compare the scale of red tints in the tomato color with the series of notes of the guitar. He might slice up the guitar form in his creation, or play a tomato. (What does a tomato sound like?) By pushing out from the particular, the ordinary, making shape studies of different sounds, he could discover new realms of possibilities, new realms of feeling, and his vision would broaden, his imagination find new dimensions. The artist as a model can inspire the high school student into a search for visual and aesthetic experiences which are vital and meaningful to him.

Contact with the professional can thus open doors to the student, showing him what art really involves, how he can deepen his own experiences, what the artist really is as a man, and what art as aesthetic experience can mean for himself personally and for society.

Art History in the High School Art Program

Courses in the history of art are becoming a familiar part of the high school art curriculum, in some cases replacing various forms of art appreciation. The art history course stresses the visual art achievements of man throughout numerous civilizations and eras. It is most often taught through historical survey or a thematic approach. The art appreciation course, by contrast, does not generally probe the origins, environmental influences, and cultural milieu with the degree of depth of the art history course. Art appreciation is better defined as an objective: a desirable outcome of art history and other courses.

Until recently, the history of art was offered only in colleges and universities, with few exceptions. One must ask the question: what is the rationale for teaching art history at the high school level? Obviously if the purpose of the course is to prepare college-bound students with a better background for their future academic work, it is a luxury few schools can afford. If art history is to be a relevant part of the high school curriculum, it must be an essential for the education of all students.

The high school art history course can accomplish several desirable goals which are relevant to every student. It can help him 1) respect his artistic heritage; 2) make valid and reasonable aesthetic judgments; 3) respect people and cultures that are different from his own; 4) comprehend the nature of the creative process; 5) become better aware of his surroundings; 6) achieve a greater personal enrichment; 7) use art knowledge in his individual and community life; and 8) learn to fully experience individual paintings, sculpture, and other art objects. Personal enrichment? Yes, but it is something to consider in a technological society which is aimed at providing more leisure time, with the resulting possibilities of an enriched life, or boredom.

Whether the art history course is presented as a chronological survey or a thematic experience depends upon the department, the teacher, and student needs. It is not necessary to defend either, for there are many characteristics common to both approaches, with each using the same organization but different emphases, in many instances. Obviously there are advantages and disadvantages to both.

THE CHRONOLOGICAL SURVEY

The chronological survey is perhaps the most logical way to begin art history in the high school. Each culture takes its position in an historical sequence, and the influences of one culture on another within an era can be readily discerned. The influence of earlier periods on later ones and hence the progression of art history can be made clear, for example the influence of classical Greek art on the Renaissance and, later, on the 18th century in both Europe and the United States. Chronologically more areas can be covered within a short amount of time, and a greater sense of continuity can be achieved because of the wide, organized view.

A chronological approach need not be over strict in progression. Cultures and works which do not fall easily within a time sequence, can be explored parenthetically. For instance, with a study of the cave paintings of Lascaux and Altamira, consideration can be given to African, Australian aborigine, and American Indian art; this might lead to exploration of children's drawings, and to insights into the works of Picasso, Modigliani, and Matisse. With a brief view of Picasso at the start of a chronological survey, students can gain a deeper understanding of his work when they reach the cubist and expressionist styles of the 20th century. As another example, American architecture can be introduced along with the study of Gothic art, with observation and discussion of churches in the United States having neo-Gothic floor plans and structural features. Likewise, a study of Greek and Roman classical architecture, can lead to a study of neo-classicism in American architecture, and then to a search for neo-classic elements and influences in contemporary architecture.

The main disadvantage to the chronological survey is that there is never enough time, especially in a one-semester course, or even a one-year course, to deal in depth with the whole history of art, and there is even less time for mini-glances into related areas. Such a course in the high school should be offered as a two-semester course.

THE THEMATIC APPROACH

The thematic approach offers more variety at one time. Themes can evolve from a study of the principles of art or from provocative topics such as Art and Fantasy, Art and War, Man and His Search for Values, Man and Nature. The approach offers a wider range of explorations, and involves many cultures and styles, as well as many media, such as engravings, oil painting, murals, wire sculpture, architecture, woodcuts, drawings. The approach is likely to be somewhat more spontaneous and intuitive, with associations, parallels, and influences being discovered during the experience and discussion of works of art.

The disadvantage of the thematic approach is the difficulty in showing continuity. Since high school students usually have no previous knowledge of art history, it is especially advantageous for them to realize the historical progression of the visual arts, and to discover connections between cultures. It is easier to compare and contrast styles and individual works, without confusion, using the chronological approach. Ideally, a chronological study, followed by a thematic approach, would be the logical way to structure the high school art history program, but time would be a difficult problem.

Both the chronological and the thematic approach can have similar instructional objectives, including recognition, terminology, comparison and contrast, differentiating and using knowledge in new situations, as well as experiencing individual works for themselves. There is sometimes a question about the relative importance of recognition of selected works of art and the understanding and application of concepts and principles. There is validity in requiring some recognition of works of art, just as there is in requiring students to develop an aesthetic vocabulary. Even a first-year medical student must identify slides of human anatomy as a beginning step toward becoming a brain surgeon. Identifying styles is also a necessary part of the art course; works of art are more meaningful and enjoyable to a student when he can make parallels and trace similarities. The Laocoön myth, for example, is more significant to him when he can trace its interpretations through Hellenistic Greek sculpture to the works of Durer and El Greco. A knowledge of the influences of one artist on another and of one culture on another are important, for such influences affect individual artists and cultures.

Although this method of comparing and contrasting has been the traditional approach to art history for years, it is still valid as one aspect of the high school art history course, for it is still a way of making works of art and styles meaningful. Comparing a seascape by an Australian Arunta tribe member to a painting by Winslow Homer, for example, can increase a student's awareness of both, and can help him understand the art expressions of peoples and cultures different from his own. Being able to differentiate the various theories of art and the varied ways in which man has created art, helps the student understand what art is and what values it has had and still has, for man.

THE SPONTANEOUS APPROACH

An unplanned approach to art history in the high school can sometimes prove to be an effective way of promoting interest. The concerns of the particular group of students, questions they may have about particular styles or artists' works, or current topics of interest such as an international or national event, can promote students' desire to explore a particular topic. Such an approach can be dynamic, but it requires very careful guidance on the part of the teacher, who must sense student concerns and yet know how to direct them. Since high school students do not have a background knowledge of art history, it is often difficult for them to know what they want to explore. Another disadvantage to this approach is the difficulty of keeping all students involved; a topic which interests some may be boring to others, and part of the group may lose interest completely. A teacher would need a very close rapport with all students in such an approach. A small group would be preferable.

THE INDEPENDENT APPROACH

An independent study of art history may be a preferred method of study for some students. Such study can be offered in addition to the regular class, as a substitute for selected areas, or as a complete course. Theoretically it comes closest to two educational ideals: self-interest motivation, and independent student-teacher relationship. However, no matter what levels of student capacity are involved the very nature of the method requires an acceptance of responsibility and skill development that reaches far beyond the conventional class. The independent art history student can organize his learning activities through a formal or an informal contract. As the student accepts the responsibility of his own direction and his own acts, the teacher's role becomes mainly advisory. He must lend critical and informative assistance, help determine that the student's goals are legitimate and realistic, and encourage relevant content. Although self-evaluation may be part of the contract, the teacher is still responsible for educational and behavioral judgment.

There are several areas of weakness that may be encountered in the area of independent study. One of these is the need for improved instruments of student identification. There is no guarantee that a student who achieves on the highest level in a conventional class and meets present identification criteria can successfully function in an area that requires so much self-direction and self-evaluation. Both the teacher and the student may not have developed skills and techniques that allow for successful independent study. Even students with these skills may lack motivation to become deeply involved in an independent study program.

THE INTERDISCIPLINARY APPROACH

The high school art history course can be presented as an interdisciplinary study, with art, music, literature, history, math, and science being brought to bear upon cultures and topics. In such an approach, however, it is important to keep the disciplines equal in emphasis, so that art and music, for example, do not become dominated by history. Team teaching can also be effective in the high school art history course, as two teachers can inspire discussions more readily by offering different points of view and varied experiences.

ORGANIZING THE ART HISTORY COURSE

The organization of learning activities for the art history class can follow the needs and nature of the particular group. Both large group meetings and smaller independent study groups should be included. Large groups are best suited for introductory background to a unit, major themes of emphasis, audiovisual presentations, individual and committee reporting, guest lectures, and formal testing. Discussions of lectures, participation in special interest sub-topics, and project work can best be handled in small groups. Individual student-to-teacher conferences and oral reporting, and student-to-student tutoring are also useful.

Perhaps introducing more semester courses that emphasize and expand upon special interest areas is desirable. In the high school a course on modern art will undoubtedly attract more students than a course on Mesopotamian art, and it may attract more students than a survey. The history of art could be fragmented into a series of mini-courses that could handle identified interest areas. Not only could ethnic interest be considered, but fresh and direct materials could be used that might be missed in the regular art history class.

In urban areas, galleries and various exhibitions beyond the established museums can offer materials for tour-oriented classes.

Relating art history to the contemporary environment and to contemporary society is another approach which can be explored. Through a study of the place of art in past cultures, the student can discover ways in which art can help improve the aesthetic qualities of the present environment, and the values which art can contribute to contemporary society and to man.

SOME SUGGESTIONS FOR THE HIGH SCHOOL ART HISTORY COURSE

Visual materials, especially slides and color reproductions, are especially important. Film strips and films are helpful for presenting some topics. Field trips to art museums and galleries to view original works of art and to examples of architecture are important in making the content of the course more direct and meaningful.

Student involvement is important. Although the lecture method is necessary for some parts of the course, discussion, student reports and presentations, and individual projects are essential for student involvement.

It can be helpful to involve some students, in creating art in relation to the art history class. Some students can benefit from developing their own art expressions growing out of experiences and insights gained through observing art expressions of other cultures and by other artists. While care should be taken that students develop their own individual expressions, rather than work "in the manner of" another artist, the desire to derive inspiration and new ideas from the study of art history should not be discouraged but given every encouragement. For example, following a study of pattern in Indian, African, Egyptian, prehistoric, Mesopotamian, Aegaen art, or any combination of these, some students may wish to create their own art expressions involving patterns they invent, possibly employing signs and symbols they create as expressions of their present-day culture.

The art teacher misses a valuable opportunity if he does not allow for such connections between the study of art history and the creation of art. However, some students may benefit more from oral reporting of a topic of interest to him, or from written work in response to a museum visit. The art teacher must keep the possibilities of the course open, and he must be sensitive enough to take advantage of student interests and insights which are evident as the course moves along.

The study of art history in the high school program should remain flexible and responsive to the students. If sensitively approached, it can contribute toward giving the high school student a feeling and an understanding for his cultural heritage and the capacity to experience sensuously and fully, individual works of art from many styles, and to derive much personal meaning and satisfaction from them. That alone would make the teaching of art history in the high school a highly valuable development.

Chapter III
ART IN THE SCHOOL AND THE COMMUNITY

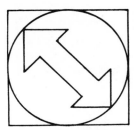

Art in the Secondary School

While what is taught, the way in which it is taught, and the philosophy of the reasons for teaching it form the foundation of the art education program, and while the teacher is the main inspiring, guiding force, there are certain practical, mechanical aspects which are essential and which must not be overlooked for achieving and maintaining quality art education. For art requires materials, space for work, and time; and these require finances. And finances cannot be secured without the understanding and backing of school administrators, legislators, parents, and the general public.

Art educators must then be concerned with such matters as the preparation and continuing education of art teachers; the scheduling, space allotments, and materials of the art program; the budget, as well as supplementary financing for special programs, artists-in-residence, and expansion of the program; and the means for affecting change, which includes such matters as legislation, political action, and public relations.

As education is a community, public, and political concern, and as art is, or should be, an essential part of every day life, so art education cannot remain separate from the community. It is only when the general public, including parents, school administrators, and political leaders, realize the necessity for art in education, and the value of aesthetic experience in life itself, that art will be truly integrated into society and that the arts will receive full support in public education.

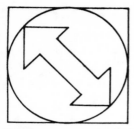

Who Teaches Art?

Every teacher is a unique individual, and teaching is a human enterprise. In a humanistic study such as art, where the content is more personal and concrete than in areas such as mathematics and science which deal with impersonal universals, the teacher's individuality is especially important. Every art teacher has his own particular vision and sensibility, his own range of experiences and values; his own way of experiencing aesthetically and of evolving his art expression; and his own way of reaching a rapport with those he teaches.

The teacher training institution, the art education program at the university level, must take advantage of such individuality and must be flexible in regard to the nature and potential of each future art teacher. For not all prospective art teachers need the same amount or the same sequence of class work, general studies, content in the special art area, teaching and learning theory, observation/participation and practicum experience, and professional studies. Some students may need a longer and more complex series of studies and experiences in a particular area than others. Some may progress more rapidly in certain areas than others.

THE CONTENT OF THE ART TEACHER TRAINING PROGRAM

The professional studies component of the curriculum includes the specialized study of the content of art to be taught to pupils, and the supplementary knowledge in the subject matter of art and allied fields that are needed by the teacher for perspective and flexibility in teaching.

The content to be taught to pupils from the field of art involves both the cognitive and affective domains. Any specific analysis of content areas requires the prospective teacher to engage in cognitive processes ranging from comprehending and applying knowledge, to analyzing and synthesizing that knowledge, and organizing it for his students. In addition, he must develop skills in evaluating the results of his program. It is further assumed that the preparation program will make a conscious effort to assist the student in conceptualizing and reexamining his values such that they will be organized in an effective system in the affective continuum.

Throughout the two major components of content to be taught, the productive (studio) and appreciative (history and criticism), conscious efforts should be made to alert future art teachers to two premises: 1) The uniqueness of works of art, from inspiration to completion is determined by the individual, his purposes, his culture, the media and tools he selects, and his methods and procedures; and 2) it is critical to develop sensitivity to, and skills in, description, analysis, and evaluation of art forms.

STUDIO

Basic concepts and skills related to processes, organizational structure, technical aspects, expressive content, communicative qualities, and technological knowledge are to be developed through studio experiences. The creation of expressive forms should include: drawing, painting, printmaking, photography, filmmaking, graphic communication, sculpture, and crafts (fabrics, wood, metal, clay, etc.). Instruction should include traditional as well as newer technological developments.

ART APPRECIATION: AESTHETICS, ART HISTORY, AND CRITICISM

The university art education program should include study of contending philosophies of art, the developments of past and contemporary art forms, and examination of theories of criticism.

ADVANCED WORK

The program should require extended work in at least one or more studio and/or art appreciation areas.

The program should not only assist the student in accumulating knowledge of the nature of art and its meanings and contributions to the individual as well as to society, but should also greatly enhance his fashioning of his personal philosophical position.

SUPPLEMENTARY KNOWLEDGE NEEDED BY THE TEACHER
FOR PERSPECTIVE AND FLEXIBILITY IN TEACHING

1. Knowledge and appreciation of related art areas: dance, drama, music, and literature including competencies in related technical and theoretical aspects.
2. Technological knowledge in areas related to the visual arts, for example, physics of light, chemistry of pigments, chemical and thermal aspects of shaping material.
3. Research, methodology, and findings in art and art education.
4. Psychology of art, consisting of contending theories, e.g., intellectualist, perceptualist, organismic, developmental stages, which consider: Differing personality types, at given levels of maturation; the apprehending and producing of art forms and various effects upon certain personality types; encountering art effects learning; and how the way in which one learns affects his apprehension and production of art.
5. Knowledge of the relevance of art to life and vocational possibilities.
6. Knowledge of the history of art education necessary as a basis for understanding current points of view.

HUMANISTIC AND BEHAVIORAL STUDIES

The program for the preparation of the art teacher should provide for the following humanistic and behavioral studies as aspects of the professional studies.

1. Sociology, so that the teacher may understand the various communities in which he might teach and understand the school as a distinct sociological unit.

    Also, the sociology of education, in order that the student be cognizant of the social dynamics of the school as a social structure, and that he be sensitive to the expectations of administration and colleagues as well as those of the community, along with his personal need.

2. Psychology, so that he may understand individual students. The future art teacher should have work in general (foundational) psychology. He should be alerted to the distinctions between personality theory and learning theory.

3. Anthropology, so that he may better understand the student in relation to his origin, environment, and cultural development.

4. The nature and aims (philosophy) of general education (including aesthetics) and their historical development in our society.

5. Curriculum, its bases, development, and the effect of change upon it.

TEACHING AND LEARNING THEORY AND APPROPRIATE LABORATORY EXPERIENCES

The program for the prospective art teacher should provide for the examination of methodologies (teaching and learning) with laboratory and clinical experience. This should include analysis and testing of theories of art education along with evaluation of the outcomes, and observation and visual presentations (e.g. films, video-tapes) to develop knowledge of various theories of teaching-learning and their application to art activities at all levels. The program should include the assessment of the intellectual, emotional, social, physical, perceptual, creative, and aesthetic growth and development of pupils as such growth is indicated by behavior of the student as demonstrated in his art product and other overt actions.

The prospective teacher should have opportunities for directed observation of and participation in art classes of various age ability and socioeconomic background followed by experience in evaluating and analyzing such situations. Such observation/participation should be introduced early, should continue through the preparation, and should be coordinated with appropriate courses, seminars, and supervision so that the learning potential is maximized. There should also be experience in developing short- and long-range goals for art learning experiences and assessing learning outcomes in relation to the realization of the established goals.

The student should have experiences in developing activities, lessons, units, curricula, and programs. At minimum, the student should have an opportunity to carry out at least one lesson (comprised of more than one activity) and if possible to teach a unit (two or more lessons).

There should be opportunities to structure and conduct experiences beyond immediate creative production, leading to the broader development of qualitative visual perception and the application of art learnings to other areas of life and school curriculum.

The future art teacher should participate in professional organizations and should gain an understanding of professionalism in the art field. His preparation should include development of the ability to communicate the goals of an art program to pupils, colleagues, administrators, and parents in an effective and professionally responsible manner.

The future art teacher should be alerted to effective ways to organize materials, media, tools, equipment, and visual aids; to manage the classroom; to attend to the learning environment; to use curriculum guides; and to evaluate the teaching-learning situation.

STUDENT TEACHING AND INTERNSHIP IN ART

The program of the art teacher should provide for a period of internship—student teaching—in a classroom and school where the student has substantial responsibility and control for the full range of teaching duties.

The prospective art teacher should have a period of internship at the level at which he will be certified to teach. The needs and personality of the prospective art teacher should be considered in the assignment of a teaching situation and of a cooperating teacher.

The prospective art teacher should be adequately supervised in his student teaching assignment by a college supervisor who is qualified by his background, training, and experience in art education. The program should provide adequate personnel, time, and funds to make possible at least two monthly visits by a college supervisor who, in addition to conducting individual conferences, will conduct seminars, and will confer with the cooperating school personnel.

The practicum situation should be one in which all involved staff recognize the need for and welcome the opportunity to join the college in the teacher preparation program.

The cooperating professional staff (supervisors, principals, and teachers), whether on campus or elsewhere, must be perceived by the college staff as colleagues in the teacher education endeavor, and must be given opportunity for professional involvement in the implementation and improvement of the entire preparation program.

The cooperating teacher should be selected because of his commitment to a practicum program, evidence of at least two years of high quality teaching, and evidence of competence in self-evaluation and growth as well as the evaluation of students. Whenever possible, it is preferable to utilize cooperating-teachers who have an advanced degree.

There should be evidence that the practicum faculty (college as well as cooperating) self-evaluates the teaching-learning process and situation while evaluating the student's progress.

The cooperating school program should utilize all community resources which will enrich the art program.

The practicum situation and active participation in faculty and organization meetings should provide the student with an understanding of the negative as well as the positive realities of the art education field, and his responsibility not only to act in this system, but also to recognize his role as an agent for change.

THE LIBRARY

The prospective art teacher must be provided with an adequate library, materials, and instructional media center.

The library should have an adequate collection of books, microfilms, and other materials pertaining to art, art education, and professional education. Recommended books are listed in *Bibliography: Art Education for Elementary Teachers* and *Bibliography: Art Education in the Secondary School,* both publications by the National Art Education Association. The library should acquire significant new books such as those reviewed and recommended in *Art Education,* and in *Art Teacher,* publications of the NAEA, and other professional periodicals. The materials and instructional media center should provide slides, audiotapes, videotapes, reproductions, films, and when possible, original art work of children. Films and videotapes concerning various aspects of teaching should be provided. Curriculum materials including guides should be available.

There should be opportunity for the high school art students to view original works of art.

EVALUATION OF GRADUATES

The teacher training institution should evaluate the quality of its graduates from the art education curriculum and those recommended for professional certification. The institution should evaluate its stated objectives and curriculum by means of a survey instrument in order to determine the effectiveness of the preparation program in terms of its relationship to the success and failure of the program's certified graduates. It should show evidence of modifying its curriculum in line with the survey findings.

ADVANCED PROGRAMS IN ART EDUCATION

Advanced programs in art education should be constructed in breadth and depth beyond that of the undergraduate program. An example of breadth could be a student's pursuing instruction in psychology, sociology, curriculum, and aesthetics because he is convinced that an art program for a deprived area must look considerably different from a program in an advantaged neighborhood. An example of depth would be a student's delving extensively into any one of those areas cited above, as well as testing his curriculum ideas in actual school settings.

Such offerings are seen as attending to not only the expanded and deepening needs of the art teacher, but also the needs of those who are concerned with art education at other points, such as art supervision, consulting, and adult/continuing education.

GENERAL CONTENT FOR ADVANCED STUDY:
PROFESSIONAL EDUCATION

The program should have advanced seminars concerned with contemporary educational problems including review of field of research, curriculum development and methodology, innovative developments, and interdisciplinary concepts.

SPECIALIZED CONTENT FOR ADVANCED STUDY

There must be specialized study of contemporary needs and developments in art, and in art education in particular.

The student should complete a terminal project indicating his achievement in depth, in a specialized area of inquiry. This could take the form of an exhibit, a thesis, a dissertation, or another form showing an original contribution.

DIRECT AND/OR SIMULATED EXPERIENCES (LABORATORY, CLINICAL, PRACTICUM, ASSISTANTSHIP, AND/OR INTERNSHIP) IN THE ADVANCED PROGRAM

There should be as comprehensive an assessment as possible of each candidate's abilities and potentials, with program structuring on and off campus for the maximum mutual development of his abilities and progress in art education. In an internship program, there should be direct or simulated experience related to the position for which the candidate seeks preparation, and continuous assessment of progress, and program modifications matching the student's development.

THE LIBRARY FOR ADVANCED PROGRAMS

The library resource should provide access to volumes of research, journals, periodicals, dissertation abstracts, and historical or classic publications in the area of specialization as well as in related areas.

THE PHYSICAL FACILITIES FOR ADVANCED PROGRAMS

There should be available standing gallery and resource funds for exhibitions of works by students, professional artists, and museum collections; a computer center for research; studies or private work areas for graduate students; and laboratories and facilities designed specifically for studies in studio and experimentation in art education and for the production of audiovisual aids and other professional materials.

THE TRAINING INSTITUTION FACULTY FOR ART EDUCATION

Full-time faculty members should have full status as college staff members and should meet all standards for preparation and experience generally held by the institution and administrative unit. The art education faculty member must have evidenced his commitment to teaching through: his responses to student interests and needs; his understanding of past and contemporary developments in professional education, art, and art education; and his participation in local, state, and national professional association activities. The faculty member must have earned a minimum of a master's degree and have attained experience appropriate for his specific teaching assignment. The college or institution should promote the professional growth and advancement of the art education faculty and offer its members full status regarding tenure, promotion, and rank, as well as all other conditions of employment. Where equivalence policies are operative in regard to rank, promotion, and tenure for studio teachers, art educators should have equal rights within those policies.

The faculty should constantly evaluate and revise their teaching, materials, and activities as they relate to the total program. The teaching load responsibilities relative to faculty activities should be in accordance with the nature of the job to be done. The faculty load for the college student-teacher supervisor should be no more than one hour credit per student-teacher. If student-teachers are at great distances from the institution location, the teaching load should be adjusted accordingly. Each member of the student-teaching team—the cooperating teacher and the supervising-teacher—should have a clearly defined position and should understand what he is expected to do. The faculty should be guided in their conduct by the code of ethics accepted by their field.

STUDENTS IN ART EDUCATION

Recruitment and selection of teacher candidates in art education should receive continuing attention. Candidates should be individually screened and selected by the art education faculty, in addition to meeting the institution's usual standards for admission. A continuing program of screening and evaluation should assure that only qualified candidates are continued in preparation programs and that students develop professional goals and attitudes. At every level of admission of students into the art education program, the total goals and potentials of the individual should be assessed.

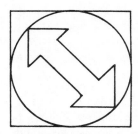

Time, Space, and Numbers in the Senior High School Art Program

It has been said that the learning environment of the public school is different from that which most artists and art teachers enjoyed when they were trained; and it has also been said that art programs should be organized by artists and taught by art teachers. Somewhere in between the existing environment of the public school and the former two statements is a workable atmosphere where every school program can achieve solid artistic and aesthetic educational goals. This section outlines some of the options available that organize the time, space, and numbers games of the milieu called the public school.

While political action for change from conventional rigid scheduling to more flexible scheduling and independent study may be desirable, the implementation of any program is framed by the existing system. The keys to stretching these bounds and making taut the program of art instruction are the teacher's pantry of possibilities and his palate for designing within the structure. It is also noted that the problems and obstacles to acceptable achievement in required art classes where enrollment is thirty-four adolescents of varied interests, must be different from those of a homogeneous group of fifteen to twenty-five who have elected to pursue the subject. But given the objectives and having the will to do so, one can explore the juggling of personnel, space, ideas, and numbers of children to the advantage of the art instructional program.

Team teaching, an educational ploy where two or more teachers lend their expertise to the same group of children, is probably the easiest adapted to any situation. It can be of immediate value to teachers of required art courses. It needs only two teachers having their classes meeting at the same time in a place big enough to hold them. The rest depends on the adaptability and inventiveness of the teachers.

As a combined group, demonstrations, lectures, and film study by both teachers can add variety and depth to the presentation; or one teacher can teach the area in which he has more depth, interest, or feeling. Using one teacher for the combined group leaves the other teacher free for planning and preparation, or busy with the logistics of the "empty" studio next door. The lab can be "scheduled" as an open studio which serves the manifest advantage of being "used."

In other adaptations, each teacher can teach his specialty in a two (or more) week mini-course, e.g., photography, perception, etc. One option would be for the instructors to exchange classes; another could give the students a choice of selecting either offering. The latter would give the students at least one choice, this being a 50% improvement in election over conventional treatment in required courses. Team teaching provides an appropriate place to bring in outside artists, craftsmen, and critics.

Open studio is a condition where a classroom or studio is open to students (or faculty, for that matter) who have unscheduled time, and where an art instructor is available for consultation. A variation of this is an advanced course in any area where only the honor students are enrolled and can come at any time. Students can continue or complete work, do other than prescribed assignments, and work in depth. It gives them a chance to vent their interests, develop new ones, and develop the ever-increasing concommitant responsibilities that go with individual study and freedom. While associated with modular scheduling and independent study, the open classroom is not necessarily dependent on a modular school system. Modified versions can be developed through making use of the team teaching approach utilizing combined classes, freeing one classroom and instructor, and allowing students to come during their "free" study periods. On a small scale, the idea of having students come in at other than assigned times already is a long established practice for students who have work to make up. The difference is to extend this opportunity to more students. A possibility for working this into existing rigid programs, provided there is an open art room, is having the art teachers freed from other duties such as study, hall duty, etc. This involves administrative support and cooperation of art staff.

Modular scheduling is a system of flexible scheduling based on a module—a period of time from fifteen to twenty-five minutes—and where structuring approximately thirty-five percent of the weekly school time is the responsibility of the student. Compared to the conventional fifty minute, equal length periods, the modules can be used individually for presenting a lesson, or flexibly grouped, several together, for a laboratory period. Modular scheduling provides the teacher a way for using time periods more efficiently. It gives the student more independent study time, permitting him to participate, as his interests and needs dictate, in open studio. It is coupled with several modules weekly of structured time. Modular scheduling is contingent upon administrative programming.

Differentiated staffing is a selection or deployment of instructors based on their area of specialty, e.g., ceramics instructors would teach clay studio. Intradepartmentally, these could be worked out among the staff for mini-courses and team teaching situations. Specific assignment of specialists requires studios and equipment strictly tailored to the area. However, the specialist instructor, having a greater abundance of ideas and experience in his area, is likely to be able to tailor ready-made space and equipment with perhaps a minimum amount of money or a staggered plan for obtaining the essential equipment for teaching in depth in his area. In a complementary version, instructors using their particular talent and interest could be part of culturally centered auditorium presentations to other groups, including parents and staff.

On a broader scale, the art teacher can become the entrepreuner of a culturally or fine-arts oriented auditorium series selecting from the staff and from the community those personalities and ideas that would stimulate and contribute to the general education of the children, staff, and community.

Independent study is an opportunity for the exceptionally gifted students to work independently and in depth in their field of specialization in courses designed for or by them, with most of the direction and evaluation coming from the student.

Each of these ideas expressed above represents organization or redeployment of staff or students to reallocate space or provide for further individualizing or intensifying of instruction. They are schemes, ploys, and ideas to be considered in renovating existing programs or in planning new ones. The following are some considerations for planning instruction.

"In grades 9 through 12 a student should be able to pursue art both as part of the general education program and in specialized electives studio courses and/or art history courses of greater depth."

Required art. In a time of secondary school upheaval, long concerted practices of giving students a panorama of the field including experiments in a plethora of media, and rather rigid teacher direction that in unison lead every student through the same art environment seem less urgent and absolute. With accent on the solo performance and giving the student more liberty in election of studies (with corresponding reduction in required subjects), the traditional structure within the concept of required art must become flexible, must broaden, and in the process, must be differentiated, allowing for mini- or sub-election by the student of intra- and interdepartmental mini-courses in various areas of studio art, art history, and humanities.

The four aspects of seeing and feeling visual relationships, the study of the works of art, the making of art, and the critical evaluation of art need not be lost or neglected. They need only be deployed or correlated. For example, a sub-elected course (within the broadened concept of required art) on the study of film or industrial art could include all the aspects, or feature one. If necessary, there could be a mini-requirement (of two weeks or more) in design, perception, etc. The difference between the sub-elective concept and traditional learning-by-units-plans is that the sub-elective is chosen and not part of a string of required units every interest must endure. (Compartmentalization will be no greater than that suffered under the traditional system.) As for planning the lessons, given team teaching or differentiated staffing, the teacher separates and adjusts the appropriate content from his sequential and non-sequential repertoire, labels it, and gives the student a choice. Given a shorter time span, and a mini-goal, the teacher is more likely to use what works best, discard unproductive holdovers, and explore timely, emotionally exciting, moment-of-inspiration goals and techniques that a strictly sequential program often blocks in a conscience-stricken teacher. Interdepartmentally, film study (not to be confused with filmmaking) and humanities should be included as a team teaching situation among the "required" choices. Art should be the core around which these courses are built. To say it in another way, the ideas, the process, and the aesthetics (the art) common to these interdisciplinary studies should be the base of their instruction.

Depth programs. Courses in which one area of instruction is carried on at a time in space appropriately equipped, and in which the instructor teaches his area of specialization, support current developments and motivational schemes. Rather than dealing with the broad spectrum, the teacher and the student concentrate on developing behavioral goals, skills, and sophistication of concept in one area that is applicable to non-verbal understanding of the abstract qualities we are often reluctant or unable to identify as the content of art. Rather than merely being conversant with the obvious and measureably achieveable concepts which are largely descriptive in nature, e.g., the elements of art, the student works within one area, gaining the experience necessary for him to relate to his area and to become aware. Through this approach he learns to appreciate process as an aspect of art.

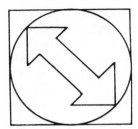

Change in Art Education

Who presses for change? Americans have been a practical people in matters related to education. If society deemed it necessary to possess a college degree to enjoy and direct societal benefits, education responded by tracking youth who matched the mold. The children, of course, facing parental wrath if another direction were chosen, played society's game. Sputnik happened, and education responded to the challenge by attempting to produce scientists out of kids who would rather repair automobiles. Chided by government, by institutions of higher learning, and by the scientific community, education geared up to surpass the Russian feat and retain America's place in technological leadership. Funding for the massive assault was provided by a concerned government which passed legislation for that end. Today the results of the assault can be seen in the lack of sensitivity toward non-material values which lost heavily and are still losing in some areas in favor of hard studies.

If advocacy for the arts has learned anything, it must simply follow the tactics of the "hard sell" for their respective disciplines. Deluding ourselves into thinking a miracle—art education in every school because it is good and wise, will never accomplish much. We have already spoken, softly at first then louder and louder, but practical education—relevant education—has a tendency to agree that art is needed, and then fire the art teacher in favor of budget considerations. A raw deal? Certainly it is. Generally, education's concern has been in the areas of materialistic gain and competition rather than learning through discovery of "who I am and what can I do best" with human sensitivity. Such learning indicates a radical change in behavior and valuing, and it is learning through art that can best produce those changes. But how? Someone has to provide the stimulus, and someone must provide adequate funding support for them.

At first glance, it would seem that concerned professional organizations would be the best choice for sustaining pressure for the inclusion of art in the curriculum. They have been doing so for years, but with priorities in education taking other forms. These organizations' pleadings have largely fallen upon deaf ears and shallow promises. The organizations will continue to pressure for change, perhaps more than ever, but they clearly need alliances, and one of the strongest is the parents of the children in art-impoverished school systems.

Parents, who ultimately pay the bills for all kinds of education, can form a powerful advocacy group for the inclusion of art at the secondary and other levels of education. In one way or another, parents elect school board members, pay teacher and administration salaries, construct facilities, and cry alot. They also elect federal, state, and local officials who are to represent their collective views. A ploy then, is to educate parents into the value of art in both their own and their children's lives. How might such a fantastic and unrealistic strategy be accomplished?

A logical step would be to saturate the media, particularly television with a proliferation of art offerings. Such a strategy would have an expressed purpose of dispelling the fears and suspicions practical Americans hold for the arts. Their attitudes are that art is for an elitist group and that it has no value in everyday living. On the contrary, parents, and especially PTA groups, must be made aware that art has value, that their own lives can be immeasurably enriched by understanding and involvement in them, and that they provide a viable alternative to this present madness called "the good life." Understanding and involvement just may make them more human. If parents could thus benefit, surely they would desire the same for their children. They would certainly demand it of their elected representatives.

Popular magazines such as *Life, Newsweek, Time, Reader's Digest, Ebony* and the like could contain palpable articles by the leading scholars in the field in conjuction with their usual place in professional journals. The point is, every outlet that could disseminate relevant information should be utilized. Television, with its wider appeal, may be a best bet in this area.

In pressing for change for art in secondary education, it would seem that professional advocacy groups might expand and combine their resources for maximum effectiveness. Concentrated power, rather than visual art, music, theatre, and dance doing their separate thing, is what change-agents understand, hence the emphasis on arts education. State and local education agencies, curriculum coordinators and planners could then be held more accountable to what they say, but often fail to do. Their thinking could be better channeled toward more humanistic education.

Colleges and universities also have a stake in moving in this direction. If art is to improve the quality of life, teachers need to be retrained so they can better serve the needs of their students and society. These same institutions could revamp their curriculums with arts-related courses in much the same way that science did in the past two decades. Pressures might also come from voices within local community itself. In some areas of the country, notably in California and New York, community art centers are providing art training for secondary and elementary children. Thus, there exist two potential voices for the inclusion of more art in the schools. One, from those persons working as instructors and administrators, and the other from the group that the centers most intimately touch—the children.

In summary, pressures for art in secondary education should come from federal, state, and local governments and educational agencies, combined professional organizations, mass media, particularly television, and from perhaps the most potentially powerful group of all, parents, local and state PTA's. The last group might provide the impetus, if they could be taught to understand and believe in the value of art education to themselves and their children.

Who pays for it? Just as pressures for change were placed at the local, state, and federal levels, these same forces would share the costs of implementing art programs at the secondary level. The logical level to share the brunt of the funding costs would be the state governments via the federal government. Various titles under the Elementary and Secondary Education Act of 1965 have already provided "seed money" in excess of 100 million dollars since its inception, and if amendments could be added that would specifically set aside X number of dollars for developing, programming, and implementing art in the schools, a chronic problem—that of financing the art component or core—would be eliminated. It is clear, however, that such will never occur unless pressures are brought to bear in the right places, hence the previous emphasis upon educating voting parents.

Another strategy might be to have art education chosen as a top priority or "a national educational objective." For example, the ESEA was amended in April, 1970, which gave the Commissioner of Education the authority to authorize special programs to local education agencies for the purpose of contributing to the "solution of critical educational problems common to all or several states." Certainly art education has produced enough research and exemplary programs that pose some solutions to critical educational problems. Advocates for art education at *all* levels might then make overtures to the Federal office for priority consideration for their discipline. The states, however, would still be responsible for administering the bulk of Federal funds for various programs. It is at this level where more expedient use might be made of existing titles under the ESEA for art education. Other federal legislation such as Title III of the National Defense Education Act, and federal agencies such as the components of the National Foundation on the Humanities, the Office of Economic Opportunity, and the Model Cities component of Housing and Urban Development may provide some service through their respective education programs. The point is, no Federal agency should be overlooked in terms of financial support. Neither should private foundations.

Watch-dogging and door-pounding could well be one of the principle functions of professional arts organizations, especially those based in Washington. As was pointed out in section one, education in the arts might better be accomplished by concerted organizations.

At the local level, art educators might use their collective powers of persuasion to influence boards of education who in turn might influence principals and administrators into providing more funds for including more art in the secondary curriculum. The "hard sell" by art educators might be in the guise of well-developed speeches and lectures before civic groups, women's clubs, business meetings, and the like for maximum saturation of ideology. These exercises would be primarily vocal, while the visual aspect of the arts could be spread through coordinated exhibitions within the community. Many dedicated art educators have been doing those things for years, but if art is to receive the kind of support it needs, more of the same, in many different places, is needed.

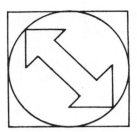

Who Pays for Art Education?

LOCAL/STATE/FEDERAL SUPPORT PLUS
PRIVATE MONEY SOURCES - FUNDS

The entrance of Federal interests into the cultural scene in 1965 was of paramount importance because that action decisively thrust culture into the center of American life. It was the final step of an evolutionary process. It was done with the support of business, science, and labor as these elements reflected their growing concern for increased leisure time. However, the presence of the National Endowment for the Arts should not mean a subsequent relaxation on the part of other public and private sectors. The states were prompted by the federal program to establish arts councils.

Arts councils, by cooperating with the schools, can help develop broad arts educational programs. By effectively cooperating with teachers of the arts, coordinating the mechanics and communications necessary to transport children to arts institutions, and artists into the classrooms, for example, the administrative burden on our over-loaded school systems could be considerably eased. Even more important, however, the efforts of an arts council in bringing together school authorities and professional arts directors can result in coordinated educational programs using the best resources in all institutions involved. The use of professional artists in school programs not only opens new vistas for both teacher and student, but provides expanded employment opportunities for the artists.

New programs are stimulated. This is similar to the reinvestment of business capital or the development of industrial research programs.

Increased cooperation which involves the artist more directly with the student is a responsibility and a concern of colleges as well as elementary and secondary schools.

Here is where the attitudes and interests of tomorrow's audiences can be stimulated, encouraged and, in fact, formed for a lifetime. State universities, strategically placed, are developing successful and meaningful programs. When one adds to this arts activities in our private colleges, a huge reservoir of opportunity exists. Increasingly, these educational institutions are recognizing the fact that while they have a responsibility to provide an education for the students who come to the campus, they are, at the same time, an influence in the region in which they are located. This is especially true in the fields of theater, music, painting, sculpture, dance, and crafts. Added to this is a concern for quality educational television programs, films, and the research and development in new art forms. A real opportunity exists for our colleges and universities to join hands in ways never previously realized, with adult community organizations in the arts, to dispel forever the old suspicions of "town and gown," and to provide a revitalization for our cities as well as our educational institutions only realized through such cooperative planning and programming. It is significant that new college facilities for the arts are being built so that programs in music, theater, art, and dance can develop cooperatively in the sharing of these facilities.

The arts are an important factor in an area's economy. Facts and figures which have been collected have, on more than one occasion, furnished helpful assistance to corporations seeking to expand in a given location or establish a new plant.

Corporations are beginning to realize the importance of supporting activities in the arts on both a local and national basis, as a forward-looking policy of enlightened self-interest. They could well become tomorrow's most important arts patrons, supplying not only money, but also talented manpower and services.

Corporate support of the arts, which is new money for the most part, will increase as the corporate managers are impressed with the management abilities of arts organizations, as well as their artistic offerings. The language of planning, research, market studies, cost analysis, and customer service applies here, and certainly is understood by the prospective corporate donor. He may have some difficulty in defining the arts and their role in our lives today, even though he may be increasingly aware of their importance, but he can certainly understand and recognize a well-administered arts organization. Only when the local arts organization has done the best job possible in managing itself, in setting artistic goals and standards, and in showing that it recognizes its total community role, can that group expect corporate officials to contribute corporate money, or the time and talents of company personnel.

Obviously, a first-class selling job is demanded when seeking corporate support for the arts. There is a growing recognition, however, on the part of corporate leaders that the corporation is truly a citizen of the community and has responsibilities to its community, as has the individual. Recognizing this responsibility, the corporate official will often want to know in what way his company will receive a return on the contribution.

There are two types of dividends which can be pointed out: the value of the programs of the arts organizations to the employees of the company, and their

70

actual participation in those programs can be all that is needed to secure the contribution. In a long-range view, money spent on the public interest—which can often mean enlightened self-interest for the corporation—will provide a satisfying return.

Business for many years has handsomely supported health and welfare activities and in the post-war period has become a significant source of financial support for our institutions of higher education. As these programs become stabilized and as departments of government increase their support of health, welfare, and education, it is only natural that business should look to the field of the arts, a major area in which it has not yet been significantly concerned. The federal government has recognized the role of corporations as donors in these several fields by permitting corporations to contribute up to 5% of their earnings with tax relief.

One of the more exciting, as well as controversial, areas of support for the arts is found in programs at the federal level. These are contained in the Office of Education's Title III of the Elementary and Secondary Education Act of 1965, and the initial programs of the National Council of the Arts created under the National Endowment on the Arts and Humanities Act of 1965.

Efforts of the National Council have been directed toward creating new opportunities for arts, launching new projects, expanding audiences, and assisting arts organizations. Grants have been made to novelists, poets, painters, filmmakers, sculptors, composers, promising graduate students in the arts, choreographers, biographers, and playwrights. Efforts to expand audiences have resulted in support for national touring companies, international conferences, arts programming on educational television, technical assistance programs, and arts in education programs.

While attention has been focused on the arts activities of the Office of Education and the National Endowment, it is generally overlooked that other government programs are available to assist the arts. While the cultural exchange program of the State Department is fairly well known, many don't know that the National Park Service offers courses for museum administrators, or that the Department of Defense makes available its arts collection to communities. Even the Office of Economic Opportunity has funded several programs involving the arts. There are a number of federal programs providing funds and services for artists and arts programming.

Washington and the Arts, A Guide and Directory to Federal Programs and Dollars for the Arts has been published by Associated Councils of the Arts (ACA), 1564 Broadway, New York, N.Y. 10036. The book covers all the Federal programs of funding and services and adds some helpful information about Federal Regulations which affect the artist in many ways. It also includes advisory groups and names of key people at all levels.

Readers are cautioned that a Federal program does not mean funding is available in the program, nor does it mean that available funds will be forthcoming upon application. In most cases, these programs represent a remote possibility of

71

funding under the proper circumstances. But it's all there; a description, eligibility, where to apply, legislative authority, and whether funds have been in the program recently and how much.

In 1969, the Office of Education (OE) transferred $100,000 to the Arts Endowment for a pilot project in which six visual artists were put into schools under a grant awarded to the Central Midwestern Regional Educational Laboratory, Inc. This money, from Title IV (regional laboratories and research and development centers) of the Elementary and Secondary Education Act, marked the beginning of the artists-in-the-schools program.

The modest transfer was followed in 1970 by a $900,000 transfer from OE that brought the program into 31 states. But in April of '71 the $750,000 that carried the program into 44 states was funded solely by the National Endowment for the Arts.

OE's $100,000 transfer was described as an expansion of a $1 million fiscal 1969 program under the Education Professions Development Act (PL 90-35) to develop arts-centered curricula and teacher-training in five pilot schools. This project IMPACT (Interdisciplinary Model Program in the Arts for Children and Teachers) restructured curricula around the arts and resulted in a situation that enhanced the entire curriculum with effects not only on the art input to children but on the other areas of study as well. In 1965 educators and arts managers saw from the start that Title I (aid to the disadvantaged) and Title III (supplementary centers and services) were going to help them develop joint programs.

These titles did help, as did Title IV.

But there are other legislative sources to tap. How effectively they are tapped depends on the response of the administering agencies and your effectiveness, along with the effectiveness of the state Arts Councils in going after this money for this purpose. Here, then are programs worth considering:

* EPDS-Section 504 (A-4) calls for "encouraging artists, craftsmen, artisans, scientists and persons from other professions and vocations, and homemakers" to teach part-time or temporarily. Section 505 calls for consultation with the National Foundation on the Arts and Humanities to plan such a program. So it is clear that Congress cut out a role for EPDA in this area.

* The Demonstration Cities and Metropolitan Development Act of 1966 (PL-89-754). Discussed in Vol. 1, No. 2 of *Education Funding News.* This act provides matching money that can be used to fund art programs as part of the Model Cities education component. It is a little used facet of the Model Cities program.

* The Cooperative Research Act of 1954 (PL 83-531 amended by PL 89-10). It was from OE's National Center for Educational Research and Development, which administers this act, that the $900,000 was transferred to the arts endowment in 1970. It pays for the experimental

school programs. You may be eligible. The act supports research to improve community involvement.

* The Appalachia Regional Development Act of 1965. These acts provide money for the rehabilitation of depressed areas, and they're especially promising in the field of arts and crafts.

* The Federal Property and Administrative Service Act of 1949 (PL 81-152). This is the surplus property program. Artists working in the schools need equipment, and this is an ideal source for inexpensive equipment.

* The Environmental Education Act of 1970 (PL 91-516). Landscaping, land use, restoration projects—whatever gets across the ecological crisis message—can be related to the arts.

* The Division of State Agency Cooperation in OE's Bureau of Elementary and Secondary Education provides funds under the NFAHA to strengthen arts instruction. Applications for this money, usually used to buy special equipment, audiovisual machinery, and textbooks, and to remodel rooms, must be submitted to the state department of education, which gets the money under a comprehensive plan approved by the federal division . . . which suggests, again, that the inventive programmer has more than one source to tap.

* Other prospects include the various programs of the Office of Economic Opportunity, operating under the provisions of the Economic Opportunity Act of 1964.

In considering the national scene, the amounts of federal money available to the arts are quite small, and this has been intentional. Federal support of the arts should not become a major factor in arts programs, and the best way to use federal funds in this area is to stimulate, help initiate, and provide minimum encouragement without in any way dominating an arts program.

Equally concerned about the role of the arts today are political leaders such as Governor Nelson Rockefeller of New York. Rockefeller recently stated,

"The arts involve people with each other and their surroundings. As such, the arts are a critical measure of "The quality of life—" a fact that historians, if not always politicians, have recognized for centuries. And as politicians and governors, we are constantly faced with combating the negative, inherited problems that have become too much for any other segment of society to handle—drug addiction, crime and poverty to name and few. The arts offer us the rare opportunity to further something that is positive—the expansion of human capacity and the pursuit of happiness—which is, after all, not only the central element of the arts, but of good government as well."

The proper use of 20th century communication facilities could do much to increase our audience for the arts, now estimated at only 4% of the population. Art and technology can join hands and benefit small towns as well as big cities in the process. Cooperative programming, cooperative funding, and a new community-wide concern for the arts can make the work of our arts organizations much more meaningful. More arts events should be held in tents, parks, public building lobbies, and schools. Those involved in the arts must make a greater effort to break the traditional mold and go where the people are.

The character of American cities is changing rapidly. The city as a setting for arts experiences is a state of mind, to be cultivated by civic and arts leaders alike. We need to re-introduce drama and excitement and an attractive environment back into our towns and cities. Special attention should be given to comprehensive arts program for low income areas, and to comprehensive arts programs involving the city and the university. A major problem must be faced by our large professional arts institutions, primarily in the performing arts, whose basic philosophies and pricing structures place most performances beyond the reach of over 90% of the city's population.

Today it is economically and technologically feasible to rebuild our cities with a sense of style and beauty rivaling the best of the past; however, no analysis has yet been made or assessment taken on the growing attempt by private and public organizations to improve the quality of city life. Concern, not money, is the essential ingredient if our cities are to survive as one of mankind's crowning achievements, instead of a monument to technological pollution.

The forces put in motion, the National Foundation on the Arts and Humanities, the programs of the U.S. Office of Education, the state arts councils, the new interest of private support resources, all will continue to have an impact in the future. As these positive elements mature with the years, their influence will grow and at the same time, because of the diversity, will allow the artists, art education and art institutions the freedom necessary to create a culture which truly reflects the values of the society.

Art in the Community

As each human being learns in an individual way and at an individual rate, alternative methods of education are obvious and necessary ways of attempting to solve our present educational problems. Realizing that the traditional methods used in present schools may not satisfy all students' needs, increasing numbers of public and private institutions are setting up new options in learning. Varieties of alternative programs are equal to the number of institutions involved, but most share the concept that optimum learning occurs when the student has the freedom and responsibility to choose and construct his own learning experiences within a supportive environment. How each school works toward this goal is that program's unique problem.

There are a number of alternative approaches to art education which have developed in recent years, as ways to broaden and enrich the art program and to bring all aspects of the community cultural life to bear upon art education. Among these innovations are the artist-in-residence program, the museum program, the art mobile, the school-without-walls, and the school within the school. In addition, many individual schools have developed their own unique ways of incorporating community resources into the school art program.

The interaction among the schools, museums, other cultural institutions, and the community at large is a valuable development for all concerned, and indeed a necessity if art is to be a deep and important aspect of today's society and if aesthetic experience is to become an integral part of contemporary life.

The Artist as a Resource

With few exceptions, the society has imposed a way of operating on the school, and the school in response has standardized teaching practices. For centuries the teacher has been solely responsible for passing on the content of his discipline to his students. That responsibility also includes accountability for quantity of content covered rather than kind. During a school year the student is to digest all appropriate concepts usually delineated by the administration, and at the end of the course of study demonstrate his mastery of the content. This mode of operating has affected teachers of all disciplines, but specifically what has it done to the teacher of art?

No matter how professional their training or how successful their professional practices, once teachers of art enter the schools they change their behavior. They stop making art, start talking about it, and watch children do it.

For the high school art teacher the standard or average teaching load consists of five to six classes a day (or their equivalent) in 40 (or 80) minute increments with an enrollment of 25 to 35 students per class. Dealing with that many students and being responsible for the learning that takes place has forced teachers to deal with their students collectively rather than individually. Although there is an effort to structure lessons to accommodate multiple learning levels and talents, that task is so great that ultimately all the students in a class explore concepts, activities, and materials simultaneously. That is not to say that teachers are too often not venturesome. Many teachers try to let students define their own direction and work individually. But if one looks at the logistics of this approach (multiply students by classes), the art teacher could be teaching 180 different lessons every day. So self-directed individualized instruction is usually awarded only to those students who have demonstrated outstanding talents and the maturity to work independently. The rest? They never get the chance.

In addition to handling logistical problems, the teaching of art implies transmitting a concept of what the arts are about—the things and events that people (artists) produce as their way of expressing themselves. The students are encouraged to do the same—to learn about art by expressing themselves through their art productions. Thus the key factor in an art class is learning about art by making art.

So the artist comes into the school, becomes a teacher, and accepts the students as his priority. He passes on his content by assuming an established teaching pattern. By dealing with the content collectively he is able to control the numbers of students and classroom management problems. He can look across the class and assess what is being learned by the students and assumes full responsibility to that end. Through the lesson structure the students have the opportunity to individually express themselves, and the artist, now teacher, given the constraints of the situation, has directed his creative energies to the art of teaching. Is there some way that an art teacher can do all this and also continue to do what he did before he came into the school—make art?

With support from administrators, staffing of schools is taking on a more flexible character: teaching aides are being used to handle some of the logistical problems; student interns learn while helping to teach; master teachers provide substantive support and direction; uncertified experts come into the school to share their knowledge and experience with the students. Community organizations and individual resource people—museums, arts councils, artist groups, individual artists—have educational concerns and skills which they are frequently eager to share with schools. Education can and does take place in the community's institutional facilities, but it can be extended into other community locations—an artist's studio, a commercial gallery, a storefront school.

These things are evidence of an increasing awareness of the broadest meaning of education—as the best of human and community resources used in the best possible ways to implement instructional programs that will truly enlighten and enrich students.

The idea of an artist-in-residence is not a new one, but it is an approach to the teaching of art that can have important implications for art teachers, administrators, and students alike. In an effort to explore ways that an artist could be introduced into the school—in particular, into the secondary school—a pilot Artist-in-Residence Project was conducted by the Aesthetic Education Program at CEMREL, Inc.[1] during the 1969-70 academic year. The project was supported by the National Endowment for the Arts with transfer funds from the U.S. Office of Education.

The rationale for the project and its documentation[2] was to explore and define operational models of an artist-in-residence program that could be generalized and implemented in other school systems. Certain initial assumptions were made. The first was that the project should reflect its national scope in the geographic, ethnic, and socioeconomic variety of the sites selected. Thus, high schools in San Diego, California; Philadelphia, Pennsylvania; West Palm Beach, Florida; University City, Missouri; and Evergreen, Colorado, were selected as well as a junior high school in St. Paul, Minnesota. The second assumption was that the artists selected should represent a range of accomplishment and recognition—young emerging sculptors as well as nationally recognized painters, a sculptor, and an enamelist were among the artists-in-residence. The third assumption was that the methods for intervention into the schools be complementary to the existing organizational structure.

The preconceived notions on the part of the project staff included two ways that an artist could work in the schools. The first was by direct intervention (classroom teaching); the second was through an indirect role (practicing art). However, a requirement of all artists was that each set up a studio in the school building and spend at least half time visibly continuing the production of his own art work. The remainder of his time was spent exploring and implementing various ways of working in a school setting and of utilizing community resources.

Each artist interacted with the students in his studio in several of the ways outlined in the model descriptions below. In addition, human resources for learning from both within the school and from the community were used. For example, the artist-in-residence participated in team teaching with other instructors, spoke to P.T.A. gatherings, conducted faculty workshops, and brought other artists into the school to talk with students and other interested groups.

The physical resources of the school were also used—in addition to the studios, libraries and classrooms became locations for artist-student interaction. And the community's physical resources—universities, art museums, galleries, community libraries, even junkyards—were drawn upon for their input into learning about art and the artist. At the end of the school year each artist had experimented with several ways of interacting with students, teachers, administrators, and the community.

THE MODELS

The Teacher/Artist, as the order implies, put emphasis on teaching first. In this role the artist took on the same responsibilities for regularly scheduled classes as the art teacher. The artist intervened directly, assumed full responsibility for what was being taught and learned, and made sure the students were involved in making their own products. There was very little evidence that the artist did this type of teaching job any better than the art teachers already in the school. The major assets were that the students knew that their teacher was a practicing artist, and that the artist taught a specialization not already present in the curriculum. (Indeed, artists were chosen with this in mind.) The art class was taught in the artist's studio. The teacher/artist's work was displayed there, and an interested student could independently come in and watch his teacher work. If he wished, the student could arrange to work with the teacher/artist in the studio beyond the regularly scheduled class time. The teacher/artist conducted classes not only for the students but for teachers, administrators, and members of the community.

Artist/Teacher—once again the order of the title implies a role emphasis. In this model the artist's own work became the vehicle for teaching others. Teaching was much more informal in nature, and course content consisted of discussions of the artist's work, seminars on art, speculations about where ideas come from, and the artist's and students' own personal concerns. In this model, the responsibility for what was to be learned, and learning it, began to shift from the artist/teacher to the students. This same emphasis was used whether classes were taught for fellow faculty members, parents, or high school students. If any students wished to follow up initial interactions, talk more to the artist, or produce their own art products, it become incumbent on such students to take the initiative and set up liaison with the artist. High school students could either work in the artist's studio, or take ideas from the studio back into the classroom and work them into independent projects.

Artist/Catalyst—the artist's priority in this model was the continued production of his art work. The secondary role was his ability to be a catalytic agent, stimulating interest in his work and in himself as an artist. Here the full burden for learning was placed on the students. They sought out the artist and availed themselves of opportunities to gain the kinds of information or experiences desired. The products from this relationship included technical expertise gained through apprenticeship, artist-and-student produced works, discussions about art, the artist and the students' perceptions of the creative process.

Although the artist-in-residence project outlined here can and should be carried on in many schools across the nation, its deeper implications are perhaps of more interest. One of these is the potential contribution to education of the working artist. Any practicing artist has involvements in the kind of community resources discussed here—a working artist knows what is going on in the galleries, museums, and with other artists, and could bring an awareness of these resources to students. A second implication is that there *are* artists in the schools now—the many art teachers who, because of their teaching load, have devoted their full energies to talking about art and watching others make art. By redistributing teaching time, the broader potentials of these individuals can be realized and the "artist" in the "art educator" may emerge.

Thus, if more students are to be exposed to more immediate arts experiences, art educators must look more sharply at the unique talents presently in the schools and in themselves and use those talents to the best advantage of the student. Setting up liaisons with the community can bring resources into the school, while changing patterns in staffing can make aides and assistants available to art teachers, freeing more of their time for the real educational business at hand—art. The artist-in-residence is not a replacement for the art teacher. What the artist adds to the school is a human resource or living example for the student to view and communicate with. The artist is part of the subject matter that is to be taught, and "artist-in-the-school" is an approach to teaching about this content.

REFERENCES

1 CEMREL, Inc., is a national educational development laboratory in St. Louis that is funded by the U.S. Office of Education for the purpose of developing and disseminating innovative instructional materials and methods.

2 S. Madeja, N. Meyers, S. Dudley, D. J. Davis, *The Artist in the School: A Report on the Artist-in-Residence Project.* St. Louis: CEMREL, Inc., 1970, 104 pp. "See-Touch-Feel: The Artist in the School" (sound, color, 16mm, 28 min., distributed by ACI Films, Inc., New York).

In 1970-71 academic year the National Endowment for the Arts and the U.S. Office of Education expanded the Artist in the Schools programs, placing poets, dancers, actors, filmmakers and 15 visual artists in elementary and high schools in 31 different states. These two Federal agencies, working primarily through State Arts Councils, once again expanded this program during the 1971-72 school year to 44 states.

The Art Museum

There are over 5,000 art museums in the United States, many with Departments of Education employing art education specialists to make the museum visit by children, youth, and the general public more meaningful and vital. Art museums offer a rich resource for art education, as they provide the housing for the major original works of art in the nation; and many museums have highly refined, effective programs especially designed for the sensuous and aesthetic experiences of children and youth.

There are numerous excuses offered by the schools for not taking advantage of the art museum as a source of enrichment for the art program, but the main reason is lack of conviction that art is relevant to the education of youth or that the museum visit can really offer anything of lasting value to them.

One explanation for this lack of conviction is that basic to the curriculum in American schools, since the advent of public education, is the emphasis on cognitive skills: reading, writing, and arithmetic. Drawing was added to the curriculum in the late 19th century as an "aid to industry." Apparently this addition occurred after American manufacturers were shamed at an international fair due to the ugliness of their designs. Shop and mechanical drawing are still big in most schools, with most other art classes (if there are any) considered a frill, a luxury. The industrial syndrome is still very much imbedded in the minds of the public and the educational decision-makers even today. The education departments of most museums are trying to compensate for this lack by offering an enormous number and variety of programs which really belong in the schools.

As a result of the neglect and/or negative experiences in the arts, generations of visually illiterate children have grown into aesthetically insensitive adults. The decisions they have made as home owners, as businessmen, professionals, and politicians have shaped the visual quality of our environment, which in turn has effected the quality of living. Emphasis on acquiring cognitive skills, instead of effective education which includes the arts, has resulted in few people being sensitive or aware of their responsibility for the public view.

Many communities, now concerned with visual blight, are reacting in numerous ways. Large metropolitan areas solve blight by tearing down the good along with the bad, while smaller communities have set up "beautification" commissions or "appearance" boards. Appearance Boards are repugnant to artists, architects, and sensitive citizens who quite rightly object to the legislation of beauty by questioning the standards to be used, on the basis that they stifle creativity.

Art should be a part of everyone's life, for through it we learn to observe, to express, and to appreciate. In turn we must teach our children that they do have aesthetic capabilities and give them the confidence to exercise these capabilities. Along with the teaching of perceptual skills in the classroom, there is a need for children to look at the forms made by other persons. They need to be aware of such forms as they exist and must be allowed to develop a personal response. Through this comes learning on many levels.

The fine arts museum in the community is one place to start the process of learning to look, but certainly is not the only resource available to teachers. There are many subject-oriented (historical, archeological, natural history, ethnic, or religious) museums which offer items with deep aesthetic values. Very often colleges and universities have museums or galleries connected to them, and many libraries have small exhibition spaces. Some corporations show, or will show on request, the collection they own. A number of states, in cooperation with museums or private collection, have traveling exhibitions which are available upon request to communities with limited resources. Zoos, aquariums or botanical gardens offer marvelous opportunities for visual stimulation, adding a new dimension to the learning of the natural sciences. As a last resort, reproductions can be used, but because so many are of poor quality, their use is discouraged. Teachers and parents should insist that their school Boards provide the opportunities to visit institutions away from school, since nothing takes the place of the actual art object. They should also insist on more than the one annual field trip.

Although exact figures are not available, most museums find ample evidence that the majority of American school children have had only one, or at the most, two formal visits to a museum during their entire school career. Since their parents don't take them to museums, this trip usually represents a once- or twice-in-a-life-time trip. The visit usually occurs at the 5th or 6th grade level. The relative maturity of the children and the ease of making up missed school work is the rationale for choosing this grade level. Approximately 75% of these field trips are for the sake of "exposure"; 20% are related to the topical concerns of the classroom (mainly history), with only 5% for the sake of heightening artistic understanding and taste, and/or the learning of art history. Actually, groups visiting the museum should range from preschool children to senior citizens, from the mentally retarded to the gifted. There should be special emphasis on the emotionally disturbed and physically handicapped children using the facilities of the museum right along with the so called "normal" students. Each tour, of course, should be geared to the group, and each group should come back more than once.

Most art educators feel that a "one shot" trip to a museum is of limited value, unless coupled with advanced preparation and extensive follow-up. Many museums, on request, will send someone out to the schools to give advance instruction, or teachers can do this themselves. Vitality and enthusiasm are prime requirements, being the major ingredients to a successful experience. Enthusiasm on the part of the teacher is as important as listening and observing while at the museum. These observations become the basis for the follow-up sessions in the classroom, which often lead in surprising directions.

Ideally a museum should set the mood for one to enjoy art and to reflect on it and somehow think about it. William Saroyan once said: "The purpose of art is, to the traveling human race, an improved road map to itself." George Segal quipped "Art is a form of superior gossip." Somewhere in between is the idea that art is a document of the cultural interests of man. Too many people see art as a status symbol, or place it on a plane which they feel is beyond their comprehension. The imposing façade of the museum itself sometimes tends to intimidate the visitor, along with the hushed halls, glowering guards, and "experts" educating the public. People go to museums for many reasons; occasionally it is to see the art. Too many people read the labels, glance momentarily at the art, and push on to the next work, hoping by some magic that they will eventually "get it." The fact that most people don't know how to relate to art has to do with the tradition of insistent assurances by some art educators that certain works of art need to be "appreciated" if one is to scale the peaks of high culture. When it comes to food, everyone is expected to indulge his own taste, but with art each tends to be suspicious of his ability to make a value judgement. The "equality of appreciation" principle which causes this suspicion, operates by labeling selected art works as "masterpieces" or "high points of civilization" with repeated stress put on their "harmony of proportion" or "the spiritual power" of the piece. If this is not accepted on faith, then a flood of facts are presented to prove the point. Those left unmoved by the holy facts are uncultured outcasts or, at best, aesthetic cripples.

The idea that art is for the "cultured few" is rapidly coming to an end. This elitist attitude is rooted in the history of art patronage as well as in museum development. Kings and emperors, temples and churches, traditionally supported the artisans, but with the downfall of royalty and the advent of the industrial revolution, the base of art patronage has broadened.

The first museums in the United States were to private collections of wealthy industrialists and were composed of objects the owner for some reason found awe-inspiring. These collections, shared with the public, reflected one man's taste and purse. The next step in museum history was the founding, in the late 19th century, of the public museum as it is known today. It was usually a large impressive building housing a wide assortment of second-rate European paintings and early American landscapes. These were donated by wealthy patrons, who also appointed a director to watch over and care for their collections. This director was responsible for maintaining the myth that owning art was the mark of a cultured person and that his museum was the fountainhead for those seeking "culture."

Museums built in more recent years, after the earlier collections had been housed, did not contain specific collections, and therefore the directors and curators became art historians and buyers as well. To support the buying, museums had to have financial backing. These backers became known as trustees. They were a small group of wealthy men, who may or may not have had a specific interest in the arts, and the inevitable conflicts arose between businessmen and art historians.

Museums soon found they could not survive on money donated by the trustees alone, and many museums needed to depend on the visiting public by establishing memberships and charging admission. The museum then felt a greater responsibility to the public . . . that of educating it.

Education departments in many museums are still operating on the elitist principal described earlier, but the community-at-large has begun to raise questions about the relevancy of the policies and program decisions being made by museum administration and trustees. Whereas the elitist orientation tended to downgrade the importance of community involvement, the new trend is toward greater involvement of the public.

Most museum education programs start with own unique function or capabilities and the capacities of the museum—its collection or collections of painting, sculpture, prints, film or photography, etc., and present it to the best of their ability. The collection, along with other museum resources and services (publications, circulating exhibitions, lectures, tours, classes, etc.) should be seen for its greater potential to: excite the imagination, develop a sense for poetic imagery, provide depth and insight into visual experience; inform, document, and explain—in short, make people aware of particular ideas about works of art and their connection to other forms. It can also illustrate and demonstrate particular techniques and/or processes in which artists have engaged in creating the work of art, if this interests the public.

John T. Murphey wrote in an article in *Museum News:*

> *The only correct use of a museum education department is as a catalyst to experience. Phrased in the old adage 'you can lead a horse to water but you can't make him drink,' the collection is the water, the public (with due respect) the horse. A misused education department simply points at the water saying 'here is the water, it is five feet deep, 20 feet across and it is wet.' But a good education department induces a thirst. The effective guide (or docent as they are referred to in museums) draws attention to the thirst quenching delights of drinking water and encourages the horse to recall his own previous tastes of drinking water, no matter how feeble or long ago. The docent sets the example by taking a sip from the stream, describing its special flavor, comparing it to other streams. The docent asks the horse his own views*

and reactions to the stream. The horse is now far more tempted to drink the water than merely to sit on his haunches considering its width, depth and origins. If he doesn't take a drink from that stream, he most probably will at the next. He has been set to thinking about his own ability to enjoy water—he is developing a thirst. The key factor to an efficient education department is the amplification of a visitor's feeling rather than his knowledge. To lead toward experience rather than knowledge alone, the docent must sense the subtle relationship between knowledge and feeling with information being translated into feelings. To give out information only is incomplete and misleading.

The "new" museum recognizes that rather than being a citadel of culture, it is a storehouse of memories and a gallery of ideas.

The Art Mobile Experience

One of the most effective and popular forms of art instruction outside the classroom, is the art mobile. Loosely based on the concept of the book mobile, the art mobile, a kind of museum in miniature on wheels, is designed to take original works of art, along with instructional materials, to communities across a wide area, for the benefit of students, teachers, and the general public.

There are numerous art mobiles in operation in the United States, with others under construction. Whether sponsored by state offices of education, museums, or private foundations, they have at least one priority goal in common: the development of aesthetic attitudes, awareness, and understanding of art, by bringing works of art and instructional materials to the public.

There are numerous forms of the mobile art experience.

One "mobile gallery" concentrates on one artist at a time, for example, Picasso. It provides lectures tours, student-teacher preparatory packets, slides, biographies, and a hand-printed gift poster, but charges $40.00 per day for a minimum three days' booking, plus transportation costs from the previous town.

Another "art mobile," which has included among its exhibits works of several North American Indian tribes, is free, and also provides information kits and excellent publicity kits, but has no teacher on board and no lecture facilities.

Another extensive "artmobiles" program grew from a single unit to four units, three curators, a director, three drivers, and coordinators in 75 communities. This is a very elaborate system which could not operate without the aid of the many sponsoring organizations which are responsible for making all local arrangements including selection of the location, arranging for publicity, working with school systems, and supplying two art mobile aides to help the curator operate the unit. However, even this program is not seen as a teaching device so much as a mini-museum, complete with sales desk.

In another art mobile program, it was agreed that in addition to serving as a museum, the mobile unit should have the capability of becoming an in-service center for teachers and other persons in the community. It was also felt that the unit should be an aesthetic example in terms of construction and design and should serve as a catalytic agent in providing cultural interest in a community.

One of the most innovative features of this art mobile is the arrangement provided for in-service education. A movable wall conceals a rearview screen and chalkboard. Behind this is an audiovisual center equipped with a cartridge tape playback deck, reel-to-reel tape playback deck, phonograph, public address system, slide projector, 16mm sound projector, filmstrip projector, dual amplifier system, and a 25 position feature lighting system for sequential programming of lights and recorded tapes. Fifteen director's chairs are stored in the space provided within the unit and may be placed in front of the screen for meetings with teachers, principals, and community groups. Equipment allows for projection of slides, films, and filmstrips by remote control; distribution of audio material on the interior and exterior; announcement and recording through an interior and exterior public address system; playing of music and tapes on the interior and exterior; and development of tape material during meetings held in the unit.

Many mobile gallery programs depend on local "hostesses" who are not art trained but merely function as guides. Others have a trained teacher-lecturer who travels with the unit. One art mobile program developed a somewhat unique system utilizing art students as lecturers. Graduate art education students are trained as lecturers and receive anywhere from three to ten graduate hours of credit plus travel expenses during a tour of duty, which is approximately two months or one quarter. This arrangement provides invaluable experience for the students and frees the director to handle scheduling, publicity, travel, electrical hook-up, and in-service workshops. The in-service program for teachers has proven to be one of the most significant aspects of this art mobile, and has led to the institution of a major program of art workshops geared toward the classroom teacher throughout the state.

Unfortunately art mobiles take money, even after the unit is constructed: money for adequate staff, money for upkeep and operation of the unit, and money for graphics, publicity, and teaching materials. One mobile system designed a packet of teaching material which is used by teachers prior to the arrival of the mobile unit in the community. Teaching kits consist of a filmstrip, recording, manual, reproductions of the paintings and sculpture in the unit, posters, and brochures, which are sent to the school two weeks prior to the arrival of the unit.

Even more than money, the effective mobile gallery needs a staff dedicated to the concepts involved. Proper use of the mobile gallery can lead to revival of art interest in the school and in the community. Traveling art museums can serve as motivating factors in increasing art appreciation, awareness, and understanding in communities removed from the large urban museums.

The School-Without-Walls

Of the many and varied alternative educational possibilities developing in America today, one of the most exciting and vital is the School-Without-Walls. It releases a student from the confines of a conventional schoolroom and allows him to participate in the activity and production which a great urban center generates, and thus it fulfills the promise of education for living.

When the community becomes a classroom, education truly becomes a living and growing process. When artists, galleries, museums, and other cultural institutions offer their skills, facilities, and technical advice to high school students, they insure the continuance and growth of our aesthetic tradition.

The experience of working with an artist, exchanging ideas with people in the professions, and observing the many manifestations of art in the city are invaluable to a young and fertile mind. It is a life to art and art to life relationship.

A one-teacher/one-room art program could never compare in terms of a learning experience to the broad possibilities which would be available to the free-moving art student in a School-Without-Walls. One large city in the Midwest initiated a system of schools-without-walls, known as METRO, an experimental secondary education program under the auspices of the board of education. An educational consulting firm was involved in the initial phases of developing and operating the schools. Within two years METRO had grown from 150 to 350 students, representing a cultural cross section of the city. In order to reflect the racial and ethnic composition of the school system, a boy and a girl were chosen from each of the city's school districts. These students were picked from a lottery of about 3,000 applicants.

The school has no conventional school building, although it does have headquarters in a downtown office building that served as office space for staff, work area, resource center, and staff-student lounge.

The nature of Metro's educational program reflects the potential for learning which can be absorbed by a student in contact with real-life situations including the businesses, cultural institutions, and neighborhoods of a city. Students can learn from people with varied skills and interests: doctors, lawyers, electricians, scientists, and artists as well as skilled teachers, who can help a student use the talents of these people to gain a rich individualized education.

The Metro student is "on the move" as he participates in classes which are located all over the city. At the same time, he is directly involved in making decisions about how the school is structured and how his own education will proceed. This involvement helps the student to become more independent as well as to motivate his learning desires.

The potential for exposure to aesthetic education is wide open for the Metro student, since he has a range of classes to participate in while exploring the creative process. Some of these classes—writing and story workshop, ceramics, photography, graphics, T.V., acting workshop, creative writing, figure drawing, art and community—are already available to the high school student.

These classes are usually held in professional settings (T.V. studios, a local art school, ceramic workshops, museums, and artists' studios). The environment is a real one which allows the student to be involved in the same way that the professional artist is involved.

One of the classes called "Art and Community" is held at an art museum; it coordinates the art activities of two groups: Metro high school students and teacher education students from the museum art school. The two groups meet together once a week to participate in mutual planning and presentation of various art productions, events, and other forms of interaction which explore media, environment, perception, and communication.

Other classes which are available offer the student information about art through field trips to museums, galleries, and artists' studios. More traditional approaches are open to students interested in art skills such as painting, drawing, and sculpture. Filmmaking, T.V. production, dance, writing, drama, and music are rapidly opening up as METRO grows to include more and more affiliations with resources in the city which perpetuate the city's cultural involvements.

The "School Without Walls" concept is geared to expansion, both in the mobility of the student and in the number of classes available to him. The future of this concept depends on the cooperation of individuals and institutions in the urban community.

In the area of aesthetic education, the future of the School-Without-Walls looks promising. As resources become more available, students can study "art" in places where "art" is being born. Locations where professionals are working can be shared by young people who will hopefully discover the potential of art not only as a career but, more important, as an alternative life style.

The traditional high school *art* class is limited, even at best, in creating an environment which is natural, interactive, and nourishing for art production. Students are generally limited in *time* (40-minute periods or their equivalent), in their *observation* of working artists (the teacher rarely works on his own projects), in a *variety* of experiences (one teacher to 30-40 students), in enough *privacy* to develop self-awareness (overcrowded rooms), and in enough *group interaction* to help foster communication (school rules, restrictions, etc.).

The School-Without-Walls offers new hope in the struggle to expand and enrich the art programs in secondary schools.

The School Within the School

The school within the school is another type of alternative program being explored. In this arrangement a specific program of specialized art instruction is designed and implemented within the existing school, for the benefit of a particular group of students who are committed to a concentrated approach to art. Such a program is certain to be highly individualized, as it depends completely upon the interests of the students, and the arrangement made within the school, for their special study and work.

A close look at such a program developed within a suburban high school in a Midwest community will reveal something of the potential and the problems of such an endeavor.

It was at a spring board meeting of the school that a group of students accompanied by invited adults presented the following philosophy as a beginning toward an alternate school. The program was to be established as a school within the existing school in order to increase the options already available to students.

1. A primary goal of education is to enable young people to lead full, meaningful, and satisfying lives.
2. Education should aid young people in learning how to relate to each other, to adults, and to the community in which they live. This implies an interdisciplinary approach to problem solving.
3. No one curriculum and/or set of experiences will be meaningful to all students.
4. The student should have increased responsibility for decisions affecting himself and the learning community.
5. Learning how to learn is more important than the accumulation of facts, so that the student may continue to learn after leaving school without the aid of a teacher.
6. The subjects and disciplines which are presently taught in the high school are helpful tools for understanding, but there is a need to test and apply these subjects to the world outside the school.

7. Teachers must view themselves as co-learners rather than as "holders and purveyors of truth and knowledge."
8. The community is rich in human and educational resources which should be tapped in the education of young people.
9. Education should encourage students to be creative and original in their thinking.
10. The school should aid students in learning how to live with others different from themselves in ethnic, religious, racial, and economic backgrounds, and in political or ideological persuasions.
11. Parents should play a more active role in the education of their children.
12. The school must be flexible enough that. the needs of each individual student can be met.
13. School can and should be an enjoyable and exciting experience. Learning becomes a desire, an answer to felt need.

The philosophy was approved by the board, and then the following proposal was presented and approved:

THE PROGRAM
1. All high school graduation requirements would be met.
2. The program and the courses in it would be formulated with the assistance of students and interested parents and recommended to the superintendent.
3. Courses could involve independent study, tutorials, or group study.
4. Courses within the existing curriculum would be open to the students.
5. Credit would be determined by an agreement between the student and others involved in the course with the approval of the teacher and the department chairman in that curricular area.

ADMINISTRATION
A steering committee would include students, parents, and teachers as well as the teacher-coordinator. The teacher-coordinator would be responsible to the superintendent in the same fashion as a department chairman. The development of policy, program, and administrative structure will be part of the educational process. As in all school matters, the superintendent will have the ultimate authority for the administration of the program.

STAFFING
1. There would be one full-time certificated teacher-coordinator for the program who would be paid his regular teaching salary.
2. Certificated teachers would be recruited from the staff of the high school.
3. The number of certificated teachers would be determined by the number of equivalent-to-full-time students in the program. The student to teacher ratio would be similar to average class size to teacher ratio in the high school.
4. Teachers could be suggested by those involved in the program, but with final approval and appointment by the superintendent.

5. Use would be made of resource personnel from the community, business, professions, the arts, and industry.
6. Family Service resources would be available to the students in the program on the same basis as to those in the regular school.
7. The program will not require additional funds for its existence.

STUDENT ENROLLMENT
1. Students must be enrolled in the present high school.
2. Student enrollment would not exceed 150.
3. Admission to the program would be on a first-come, first-served basis, with students who have been active in developing the concept of the program given priorities at the initial enrollment.
4. If there should be an overwhelming interest in admission to the program, a selective, elective lottery system would be developed to insure heterogeneity in the 150 students.
5. The program would be open to all students with parental approval, regardless of year in school or previous academic achievement.
6. At least a semester commitment to the program would be required of all students except in extreme, rare cases which will be decided upon on an individual basis.
7. State attendance requirements would be met.

USE OF HIGH SCHOOL FACILITIES
Extra care would be taken to insure that this program and the students in it would not, as interpreted by the superintendent, interfere with the functioning of the regular school program.

IMPLEMENTATION
1. The initial phase of the program would begin in the summer, with a group of fifteen to thirty students who would enroll in summer school and pay the normal tuition fee.
2. A teacher-coordinator for the program would be paid according to the regular summer school salary schedule.
3. Assuming that the summer school phase implies its continuation, the experimental program would begin in the following September, with an enrollment not to exceed 150 students.
4. Not later than December, a report to the Board of Education would be made. At this time a recommendation will be made to the Board by the superintendent for their decision regarding the continuation of the program for the second second semester.

At the beginning of fall semester, students and faculty spent considerable time designing courses and directions of study. Some of the courses were unexpectedly traditional while others departed from the norm to an exciting degree. By the middle of the semester, some of the courses were either abandoned, completed, or replaced as the education process evolved. Growth was heavy with both problems and enthusiasm. Normal activities in any learning institution, such as entering and leaving the building, communicating the simplest information, handling administrative detail, making reports to parents, all became new monsters to be tamed in the new program. The program had its own peculiar problems, too: individual commitments or contracts were difficult to formulate and easy to change; most people found the enormous responsibility of personal and educational freedom difficult to deal with; the sense of community necessary for successful operation and adjustment seemed inadequate to meet out needs. However, systems were and are invented to help solve our "growing" problems.

One of the most valuable developments within the program was the establishment of team training for the staff. This was provided through a series of intense developmental workshops conducted by an expert in the field. It is anticipated that this training will continue through the first year. As the team grows in strength, it is better equipped to facilitate further student input into the program. The powerful resource of the community is also beginning to be investigated. Maximum use of all resources could very well involve years, but the process has begun.

Staffing was set up with the teacher-coordinator, four full-time teachers, and several part-time people. Some of the part-time people were certificated teachers, others were members of the community. From the beginning, art was integrated into the program through one part-time certified teacher who was released one period a day from the traditional school.

The first semester approximately one-third of the students chose to become involved in art. Their work was totally independent study facilitated and critiqued by the art teacher. Some students took art classes from outside sources, but most of the work was done based on their own resource, energy, materials, and studio space. Total program stimulation was attempted with specialized demonstrations and seminars by volunteer artists and the regular teacher. This type of exposure aroused nominal student interest. Perhaps trips to artists' studios would be more stimulating, but transportation and the number of students make the idea prohibitive for the time being. In addition to independent study, other staff members led successful integrated courses such as "Mathematics Through Art" and "History Through Art." At the end of the first semester the art program as well as the total program had stimulating ideas for the second semester.

The second semester opened in the art program with an umbrella course titled "Creativity with an Accent on Art." This approach differed from the first in that students would not only pursue their individual directions, but would also use the teacher's art room during most of the day for common studio space, and would agree to meet on specific dates for community building activities. The necessity for this structure developed from the need to be able to pull all of the students together for improved communication as well as to be able to take advantage of organized field trips.

Some of our major concerns include: improved communication between parents, students, and staff; even distribution of administrative work throughout the staff and perhaps parents; total student involvement and increasing parental involvement; further research and use of community and outside resources; and increasing the part-time staff time-allotment.

The concerns of the art program are also those of the total program, with some specific additions. We look forward to having more time available to facilitate courses such as "Art History and the Art Museum" in which the student will have the opportunity to attend the museum for conducted gallery talks and interchange on artists and their work. "Gallery" might be a title for a course investigating the differences and operations of galleries of the area. These ideas alone suggest a need to move art study out of the school confines and into community resource on a regular basis. We could easily investigate store front studios and community art potential, to put students in a more realistic studio situation either individually or in small groups. Materials will be provided through direct funding as the Experimental Program becomes a separate department within the school. By partially removing the art program from the traditional school building and by individual funding, new physical facilities such as gas-fired kilns are real possibilities.

Alternative education provides many rewarding experiences, but because of its inherent demands for total participation and dedication, not all people are capable or willing to be involved. All alternative schools have one thing in common: the decision to become involved enough to begin building a program.

The approach is highly creative. Its potential is unlimited and vast. With care and flexibility, and with sensitivity to the students and to the need for the arts and for aesthetic experience in today's society, much of value can be accomplished through the school within the school.

Art Education in
Small Communities

While many large metropolitan and suburban schools are developing extensive art programs, and while many alternative arrangements are being developed for bringing art to the community and the inner-city as well as to bring children and youth to the museum, the store front school, the recreation department for art experiences and enrichment, there remains the question of the vast number of modest high schools in small towns and communities across the nation. These high schools, closely geared to the backgrounds and needs of the local communities, often have very limited art offerings—rather traditional, project-centered courses for those few students who choose art as an elective, out of talent, interest, or the inability or lack of motivation to succeed in the other more academic work. Innovative programs are less likely to reach these schools, as the schools involve small groups of the population, and most often both the community and the school administration are content with offering the so-called academic necessities and skills needed to prepare youth for a practical life in society.

Yet art educators should be concerned for the art programs in these small community high schools, for they are in charge of the education of a great segment of American population. And it is this population which needs to realize the deep human values which the arts alone can contribute. It is this body of youth who need to be made aware of their art heritage, the aesthetic experience, and the individual responsiveness and creativity which can make them more complete and sensitive persons.

Let us look for a moment at a high school in a community of 30,000 people. The school opened seven years ago on the outskirts of the city, with approximately 900 students attending. Sixty students enrolled in art, and since this was a four-year high school, the art classes were labeled Art I, II, III and IV. After four years the art enrollment had not grown to any extent, and the art budget had been cut from $800 to $700 annually. The one art instructor had excellent qualifications, but something was wrong.

Following much consideration and months of planning, the school administration and the art instructor decided to drop the traditional program and develop a variety of quarter courses. They felt that this change would offer a wider range of experiences both in content and media. Such courses were offered as Drawing I and II, Design I and II, Introduction to Art, and Individual Studies in Art for advanced students. A program of craft techniques was also introduced. Within a year the enrollment had increased in the arts from 60 students to 160.

These new courses offered an improved means to enriched backgrounds and to life appreciation. This type of program allowed greater depth in experiences for students and a greater selection in particular art interests. Quarter courses increased student participation and provided better utilization of space, and materials. A student entering this high school as a freshman could take four or more quarter courses in art, and if he planned to become an art major in college, he could take as many as 22 different art courses by the time he was graduated. This program offered a much stronger background for the college-bound student and for the student who intends to major in art. It also offered a variety of courses for the student who was interested in taking art simply for his own enrichment.

A poll of the students after this program had been in existence for fifteen months revealed that out of the 160 students, there were only ten who were not satisfied. Most comments from the students concerning the program were favorable. One girl stated that she liked the quarter classes because they offered her a greater variety. Another commented that the quarter courses could give one the opportunity to experiment and learn more about art both in general and in depth. One young man said that he had learned more in art under the quarter system because it gave him time to experiment and learn more about one particular medium. Still another boy stated that he enjoyed the classes because when he started a new medium he lacked confidence, and the new program allowed for a longer period of time in which to gain proficiency and confidence in a particular medium.

All of the classes in this art program were basically planned to develop an original and creative approach to works of art for high school students. Individuality of thought and expression was encouraged at all times. The program led the student into problem solving experiences through the utilization of a sequential structured exploration in a variety of media, projects, thought concepts, and aesthetic appreciation.

In order for art education to survive in this small community, it was imperative that the most important objective be to teach young people the value of living a full and happy life. An opportunity for creative expression is the right of every child. To see that the child gets this right is the obligation of the United States government, national art and professional organizations, state and local governments, local school and community officials, and teachers.

The purpose of art programs in rural and semi-rural areas and small-towns should not be to produce artists but to develop attitudes toward being creative, to increase appreciation and awareness in the individual, and to help pupils understand themselves. Even the financially poorest school districts can provide many ways in which to allow students to obtain a meaningful art education. The aim of the school should not be to produce artists; the art program should provide a structure which will arouse and stimulate the desire to express and to experience, and which will contribute to the enrichment of the individual.

However, even with the primary goals of appreciation and creativity, some small art departments still face the danger of setting technical standards too high for many students. Far too many art programs are killed because the standards for proficiency are too high for the students to reach, and consequently students lose interest. Spontaneity and creativity are lost. Also, some art department standards are so high that school districts cannot afford to implement or maintain them. The art program must be built with sensitivity to the community, the particular body of students concerned, the financial capacities of the school system, and the values of art. It must be developed through a sensitive but effective rapport between art specialist, administrators, students, and public.

Since art is a significant contribution to the daily living of every individual, the senior high school should include in its curriculum, learning oportunities in art for all youth. Art should be an integral part of the curriculum on the secondary level, not only for the gifted, but for all young people, for all can use their art experiences as intelligent consumers and as human persons with a capacity to feel and to respond. Special emphasis should be placed upon planning the art courses so that all pupils may understand that art is a part of living here and how, a means of individual expression and enjoyment, and a way to the enrichment of life.

This kind of art program is especially rare in small community high schools, but it is so needed by them, for such a program which stresses individual awareness and enjoyment of aesthetic experience and individual creativity and expression, can contribute much to the lives of people. And by educating this large segment of the population to a sincere appreciation of what art can offer them and their children, much can be accomplished in helping society realize the values of the arts in education and in life.

In the particular school given as an example, the revised and more vital art program became so popular that many of the quarter courses in art were expanded to semester courses, and some to year-long courses.

Future directions for art education in the high schools of smaller communities, would be a requirement of some art for graduation; a better means of informing a public about art; the educating of counselors regarding the values of art; better scheduling for the arts; and the hiring of only the most qualified personnel to teach art.

There can be no real improvement in art education in any community high school, however, until there develops a discernible force to influence the public towards the necessity for an expanded and deepened art program and toward a realization of the values of art for every human person.

Careers in Art

We are living at a time when a great number of people are involved in creating and designing a vast array of objects. The media of communication is involved in a revolution more powerful and far reaching than any other taking place today. Television is the most powerful force in the changes that are daily taking place and that directly affect the lives of everyone, educated or uneducated, young or old.[1] The average child spends more time in front of the TV screen than with his teachers or parents, and the adult will pass from ten to fifteen years of his total life span watching television.[2] It has been estimated that the average American encounters about two thousand sales messages a day, including advertising and all kinds of visual and verbal communications. Indeed, 83% of all the information a human being acquires is acquired visually.[3]

Business organizations, labor unions, governmental entities, educational institutions, church and secular charitable groups, non-profit organizations all in recent years have become more concerned for forceful, positive identification.

Art and design are not just static bodies of material preserved intact and taught as merely a good thing to know about, a refined adjunct to the real problems of living. The average person who never spends time in art galleries and museums is daily in contact with the creative work of artists and designers. Art is a central life style that exists in the buildings we live and work in, the posters, magazines, books, and mail we read, the vehicles we ride in, the clothes we wear, and the appliances and utensils we use for preparing and consuming our food. Characteristic of our use-it-once—throw-it-away culture, most design, while it may be reproduced in vast quantities, is remarkably short lived. After only a few seconds or, at most, a month of exposure, the television title and magazine illustration pass into oblivion. In spite of this impermanence, however, the fast-growing fields of design command many of the brightest and most inventive talents in art.[4]

The secondary art program can and must be involved with the exposure of the applied arts as well as the fine arts. Many high school art programs have begun to take the initiative to get involved with the visual elements of the other school departments and extracurricular acitivities. The art program can participate in the visual execution of the school yearbook, newspaper, musicals, school decor, weekly bulletins, and classroom audiovisuals. Unfortunately, art programs in general have not been as active as the language arts programs in the class use of visual media such as movie film and closed circuit television videotape productions.

It would seem appropriate to provide an art student interested in an art career with a basic knowledge of all basic processes, tools, and methods involved in the preparation of art for reproduction, as well as experience in the illustration, layout, and design of a cover of a school yearbook. Why should students of an art class remain ignorant of how their illustrations and lettering will be photographically reproduced and printed for the school newspaper? Why should students in a graphic arts class be given an assignment to print a business card using an existing format, or with a minimum of instruction in the basic use of typesetting, be asked to layout their own design? The students in both the art class and in graphic arts class will have a better insight and understanding of the demands of an assignment if they have experienced the complete planning, development, and execution of their ideas.

The secondary art teacher should inform a student planning to enter the field of design that one's drawing ability is not the most important asset, for "anyone can learn to draw." The main concern is one's ability to formulate ideas and express these ideas clearly on paper. The job of design consists mainly of experiment, trial, and discard. The designer must work with familiar elements but design something unique.

Finally, the point should be made that no matter how good the art program at the secondary level, it cannot give youth a full and complete preparation which will serve them for a lifetime career of employment. It can and must give youth those skills, insights, and understandings which they need in order to make a satisfactory choice of schools that would best prepare them for their occupational future.

REFERENCES
1 McIlhaney, *Art As Design: Design as Art.*
2 *Ibid.*
3 Ben Rosen, *The Corporate Search For Visual Identity.* New York: Van Nostrand Reinhold Co., 1970.
4 *Ibid.*

NATIONAL ART EDUCATION ASSOCIATION
1916 ASSOCIATION DRIVE, RESTON, VIRGINIA 22091

ISBN 0-937652-04-0